SECTION OF STATE AND LOCAL GOVERNMENT LAW

RLUIPA READER

Religious Land Uses, Zoning, and the Courts

MICHAEL S. GIAIMO AND LORA A. LUCERO, AICP
EDITORS

American Planning Association
Making Great Communities Happen

Defending Liberty
Pursuing Justice

Cover design by ABA Publishing

Printed in the United States of America.

14 13 12 11 10 5 4 3 2 1

Library of Congress Cataloging-in-Publication Data

The RLUIPA reader : religious land uses, zoning, and the courts / Michael S. Giaimo and Lora A. Lucero, editors.

p. cm.

Includes bibliographical references and index.

ISBN 978-1-60442-358-7 (hard copy : alk. paper)

1. Land use—Law and legislation—United States. 2. Church lands—United States. 3. Corporations, Religious—Law and legislation—United States. 4. Zoning law—United States. I. Giaimo, Michael S. II. Lucero, Lora A.

KF5698.R57 2009
346.7304'5—dc22 2009008057

www.ababooks.org

Contents

About the Editors

Michael S. Giaimo practices land use law as a partner in the Boston office of Robinson & Cole LLP. He authored an amicus brief for the American Planning Association in the *San Jose Christian College v. City of Morgan Hill* case in the Ninth Circuit, and frequently writes and speaks on RLUIPA, zoning, and other land use law issues. He received a B.A. from Amherst College, a J.D. from Harvard Law School, and a master of city planning from Massachusetts Institute of Technology.

Lora A. Lucero, AICP, is editor of *Planning and Environmental Law*, published by the American Planning Association, and co-editor of *Zoning and Planning Law Report*, published by Thomson West. Lora is a city planner and a land use attorney with a consulting practice in Albuquerque, New Mexico. She is staff liaison to APA's Amicus Curiae committee. She is a member of the American Institute of Certified Planners and an elected member of the Council of the ABA's Section of State and Local Government. Lora received her B.A. in urban and regional planning from the University of Washington and her J.D. from Santa Clara University School of Law.

About the Contributors

Graham S. Billingsley, AICP, is principal of Billingsley Consultants. For eighteen years he was the Director of Land Use for Boulder County, Colorado. He received a Bachelor of Urban Planning from the University of Cincinnati and a Master of Landscape Architecture from North Carolina State University. Prior to that he was the chief planner for urban design for the City of Dallas, manager of the Zoning Transition Program, and principal of Billingsley Consultants in St. Louis and SFDG Consultants in Cincinnati. He has received several planning and landscape architecture awards including the national APA award in 1988 for the Dallas Zoning Code and Zoning Transition Program. Mr. Billingsley is president of the American Institute of Certified Planners (AICP), the professional institute of the American Planning Association.

Daniel P. Dalton, a founding member of Tomkiw Dalton, PLC, represents religious entities in land use disputes throughout the United States. He actively lectures, litigates, and writes on issues related to the Religious Land Use and Institutionalized Persons Act (RLUIPA). Dan received his B.A. from Western Michigan

University and his J.D. from the University of Detroit School of Law. He served as a law clerk for Chief Justice Dorothy Comstock Riley of the Michigan Supreme Court. Dan co-chairs the religious land use subcommittee of the ABA Section of State and Local Government Law's land use committee, and currently serves on the boards and committees of several other organizations, including the Society for Nonprofit Organizations, the MORE program, and the Pinnacle Forum, Michigan. He is a life member of the American Bar Foundation and a member of the American Planning Association and the Michigan Planning Society.

Marci A. Hamilton is a visiting professor of public affairs and the Kathleen and Martin Crane Senior Research Fellow (2007–2008) at the Program in Law and Public Affairs, Woodrow Wilson School, Princeton University. Professor Hamilton holds the Paul R. Verkuil Chair of Public Law at Benjamin N. Cardozo School of Law, Yeshiva University, where she specializes in church-state law. She represented the City of Boerne, Texas, before the U.S. Supreme Court in *City of Boerne v. Flores*, the 1997 case that held the Religious Freedom Restoration Act unconstitutional in the context of a land use law case. She also testified as a constitutional law expert before committees in the U.S. House and Senate regarding the constitutionality of the Religious Liberty Protection Act. Professor Hamilton has represented a number of local governments and neighborhoods involved in RLUIPA litigation and is author of *God vs. the Gavel: Religion and the Rule of Law* (2005), which devotes a chapter to religious land use.

Vivian Kahn, FAICP, is associate principal of Dyett & Bhatia, San Francisco, and principal of Kahn/Mortimer/Associates, Oakland. She previously served for nearly a decade as acting deputy director and manager of current planning and zoning officer in the City of Berkeley's Planning and Development Department. Ms. Kahn's practice focuses on preparation of land use and development regulations. She co-authored two chapters on zoning in *California Land Use Practice* (2006), which discussed RLUIPA and state restrictions on regulation of religious land uses. Ms. Kahn is a former member of the American Planning Association's National Board and is currently a member of the APA Amicus Curiae Committee.

Wendie L. Kellington is an attorney who focuses her practice on natural resources and energy law. In her land use practice, she consults with and represents religious institutions. She frequently writes and lectures on the Religious Land Use and Institutionalized Persons Act and is a faculty member of the ALI-ABA Land Use Institute. She is a member of the Oregon Bar Association and the Oregon Bar Real Estate and Land Use Section.

Dwight H. Merriam, FAICP, founded Robinson & Cole's Land Use Group in 1978. Dwight has published two hundred articles and four books, including *At the Cutting Edge 2008: Land Use Law from* The Urban Lawyer (2009) and *Eminent Domain Use and Abuse:* Kelo *in Context* (2006). His book *The Complete Guide to Zoning* (2005) has become the best-selling trade paperback on the subject. Dwight teaches land use law at Vermont Law School and is a counselor of real estate, a member of the American College of Real Estate Lawyers, a fellow of the Royal Institution, of Chartered Surveyors, member of the Anglo-American Real Property Institute, past president and fellow of the American Institute of Certified Planners, and vice-chair of the ABA State and Local Government Law Section. He has represented governments in several RLUIPA cases.

Deborah M. Rosenthal, AICP, is a partner in the Land Use and Natural Resources Practice Group of the law firm of Sheppard, Mullin, Richter & Hampton, LLP in Costa Mesa, California. She is a member of the American Institute of Certified Planners and has been active in the American Planning Association for many years. She has worked on development projects throughout California involving religious land uses, environmental compliance, civil rights, and takings. Deborah has published numerous articles on land use and development issues. She has a B.A. from the University of Michigan, a master of regional and city planning from the University of Oklahoma, and a J.D. from Yale Law School.

Patricia E. Salkin is the Raymond and Ella Smith Distinguished Professor of Law at Albany Law School, where she is also associate dean and director of the Government Law Center. Patty is the author of the five-volume *American Law of Zoning* (5th. ed 2008) and the four-volume *New York Zoning Law and Practice* (4th ed.

2008). She is the author of two textbooks and dozens of law review articles, columns, studies and reports, and other publications on the topics of land use law and government ethics. She is a past chair of the ABA State and Local Government Law Section and the current chair of the Amicus Curiae Committee for the American Planning Association. Patty received her B.A. (cum laude) from the University at Albany and her J.D. (cum laude) from Albany Law School.

Roman P. Storzer is a principal at Storzer & Greene, P.L.L.C., a Washington- and New York-based law firm that represents religious institutions in a variety of civil rights matters, and the former director of litigation at the Becket Fund for Religious Liberty. He has represented scores of churches, temples, mosques, synagogues, and religious schools in RLUIPA matters across the nation and has been described by the Hastings College of Law's Center for State and Local Government Law as one of the country's leading RLUIPA advocates.

Alan Weinstein has a joint appointment in both the College of Law and College of Urban Affairs at Cleveland State University and directs the Colleges' Law and Public Policy program. He is a nationally recognized authority on planning law issues who lectures regularly at both planning and law conferences. Professor Weinstein is the co-author of *Federal Land Use Law and Litigation* (2008) and *Land Use and the Constitution* (1989) and has authored more than seventy articles and book chapters. He has written extensively on land use regulation of religious institutions, including RLUIPA, and has been an expert witness for the U.S. Department of Justice in RLUIPA litigation.

Bryan W. Wenter, AICP, is an assistant city attorney with the city of Walnut Creek, California. His practice focuses on land use and local government law. He is chair of the Land Use Planning and Zoning Committee of the ABA's Section of State and Local Government Law. He earned his J.D. from the University of North Carolina School of Law, a master of regional planning from the University of North Carolina, and a B.A. from the University of Oregon.

Introduction

Lora A. Lucero, AICP

Land use regulation, property rights, and religion—a potentially volatile mix in any community. Add to the brew the Religious Land Use and Institutionalized Persons Act of 2000 (RLUIPA; 42 U.S.C.A. §§ 2000cc et seq.) and, depending on whom you talk to, there's either an explosion or a celebration. Some consider RLUIPA a shield to protect religious land use applicants (particularly minority religions) from the abusive, exclusionary zoning practices of local officials. Others view RLUIPA as a sword wielded by bullying applicants who want special treatment or want to avoid the land use regulatory process altogether. The truth probably rests somewhere in the middle.

There are four major participants in any RLUIPA dance—the religious land use applicant wishing to build on or use his property in some way that requires a permit; the local government authorized by the state to plan for, and regulate, land use in the community; the Civil Rights Division of the Department of Justice, with the responsibility of monitoring and enforcing compliance with RLUIPA's provisions; and last, but not least, the neighbors. Each has an interest in making sure the development review process is fair, bringing a perspective to the dance that needs to be understood and accommodated. This book attempts to explain these different perspectives with the hope that it fosters a better understanding among all participants.

This book is a RLUIPA primer for planners and attorneys alike. Any quick reading of the Act confirms that RLUIPA is *not* a model of clarity, as many federal district court judges will certainly agree. The drafters left some important terms undefined, such as "substantial burden," and created an incentive for some to litigate while providing a disincentive to others. The Act authorizes recovery of attorneys' fees for the prevailing religious land use applicant but not for the local government. So it might be fair to say that RLUIPA has brought another participant to the dance—the district court judge.

Land use and development decisions are quintessentially a local affair. No one really wants it any other way. But RLUIPA has changed—intentionally or unintentionally—the local land use dynamics, and the dance has become an outright brawl in some communities. Consider the following news items from local papers:

- Jackson County, Oregon, denied permission to a couple who wished to locate their proposed New Age church within three miles of a city's urban growth boundary. They built their eleven-thousand-square-foot home before applying for church status and for exceptions to the land use laws, which prohibit churches within the urban growth buffer zone. Rather than consider alternative sites for their church on their ninety-six-acre parcel, the couple insisted there was only one possible "power spot" for it. Their attorney said, "The question is, does the land use rule substantially burden the claimants' exercise of religious freedom? We claim it does."
- Boulder County, Colorado, denied plans submitted by Rocky Mountain Christian Church to nearly double its space to two hundred forty thousand square feet. County officials claimed the proposed structure was too large and encroached on the rural and agricultural nature of the area. The nondenominational Protestant church has exploded in growth in the past few years and has several thousand members. They want to add a gymnasium, chapel, and several hundred parking spaces. In November 2008, a jury

ruled that county officials had not violated the U.S. Constitution but had violated RLUIPA. No damages were awarded, and the decision about what permits to issue for the facility was left in the hands of the district court judge. Both sides claimed victory.

- JUDGE RULES THAT GOD IS STILL WELCOME IN MILLERSVILLE, TENN., the local headlines read. A city official rejected an application submitted by Layman Lessons, a Christian ministry formed to aid the homeless and destitute, based on a pending ordinance that, if passed, would have limited all religious and nonprofit uses on any commercial lot in the city. Layman Lessons brought a RLUIPA challenge against the city, and the district court judge ruled in plaintiff's favor. The ministry's attorney said that the ruling "confirms that Tennessee is still a place where the rights of the 'Davids' cannot be casually usurped by the 'Goliaths' of the world."
- Gainesville city commissioners voted to change the minimum lot size required for a place of religious assembly to one acre for every one hundred members of a congregation, and an additional half acre for every one hundred members after that. "If we don't take action . . . then we could get a very incompatible use in a single-family neighborhood," said one commissioner. They also passed a moratorium on issuing any future permits to places of religious assembly until other issues are addressed, such as regulations governing meals and housing for the homeless at religious institutions.
- Muskegon, Michigan, denied a special use permit requested by Celebration Community Church to hold services for its 120 members in a large, vacant commercial building. Planning commissioners noted concerns expressed by owners of two nearby bars who feared the negative consequences for their businesses, as well as concerns about taking the building off the tax rolls for use as a church.
- The Carlinville Southern Baptist Church purchased a former Wal-Mart superstore (sixty-thousand-square-foot building) in Carlinville, Illinois, and applied to have the property rezoned because the land use code allows churches only on property zoned "R" for religious or rehabilitative uses. The mayor told the local news media that the "city had

been ravaged by business closings and needed the revenue of a commercial enterprise," so the rezoning request was denied. The city filed suit in state court to enjoin the church from renovating the superstore and moving in. The church then filed suit in federal district court. "This is not about a building, and we're not just trying to win a court case," the pastor said. "We're asking God for a spiritual awakening for our entire community. Everyone in this area is paying attention, and we need God to show up in undeniable ways so that undecided masses recognize His power."

- MAMARONECK VILLAGE TO PAY $4.75M TO YESHIVA, read the headline in the local New York paper. After more than five years of litigation and $900,000 in legal fees, the village settled the dispute concerning the Orthodox Jewish school's expansion project. Westchester Day School first approached village officials in 2001 with a request to approve a new, twenty-room school building. The new structure was to be the fifth building on a twenty-five-acre campus where 450 students attend both religious and academic classes in preschool through eighth grade. The school said they had outgrown their space and would lose enrollment unless they could expand. Neighbors complained about the already congested traffic. The zoning board denied the request and Westchester Day School sued. The federal district court concluded the village had violated RLUIPA and ordered zoning officials to issue a permit for the new building. In October 2007, the Second Circuit affirmed. The settlement agreement gives the school the green light to proceed with construction, as well as $4.75 million, which the village will pay over the course of three years.
- A representative from the Civil Rights Division of the Department of Justice reported in mid-2008 that his unit has reviewed more than 160 RLUIPA matters (a "matter" being defined as staff having spent two hours or more on it) and opened forty full investigations. He reported that eighteen of the matters have been resolved with what DOJ considers to be favorable outcomes. In five cases, the DOJ has filed lawsuits against municipalities, three of which have been resolved with favorable outcomes and two of which are

pending (both of these cases are in New York—one involving the Village of Airmont and one involving Suffern). In addition to the filing of lawsuits, DOJ has filed amicus curiae briefs in other RLUIPA cases.

The *Reader* is a practical resource for each of the participants involved in disputes like those described above. We begin with the historical context. Deborah M. Rosenthal explains why the Religion Clauses were included in the U.S. Constitution and how they evolved under the Supreme Court's decisions, setting the stage for the *Employment Division v. Smith* decision in 1990. In chapter 2, Marci A. Hamilton describes RLUIPA's tumultuous legislative history. We then move into three chapters that offer different perspectives about RLUIPA: one by Roman P. Storzer, who has represented many religious land use applicants in RLUIPA cases (chapter 3); a second chapter by Marci A. Hamilton, who has represented neighborhood groups (chapter 4); and one by Wendie L. Kellington, who has reviewed publicly available DOJ materials (chapter 5).

The second half of the *Reader* is a practical resource for both planners and attorneys. Michael S. Giaimo summarizes significant RLUIPA case law in chapter 6. Dwight H. Merriam, having represented a number of local municipalities in RLUIPA litigation, provides sound advice from a local government lawyer's perspective in chapter 7. Alan Weinstein carries on this discussion with advice about how to avoid RLUIPA challenges in chapter 8. Colorado planner Graham S. Billingsley reminds planners in chapter 9 that RLUIPA is fundamentally about fairness. Chapter 10 presents the top ten tips we should not forget in the RLUIPA dance. Since RLUIPA is a work in progress, Patricia E. Salkin concludes with recommendations about where we might go from here, e.g., whether RLUIPA should be reviewed, reformed, or repealed.

Religion and the Constitution

1

Deborah M. Rosenthal, AICP

> Congress shall make no law respecting an establishment of religion, or prohibiting the free exercise thereof.

Every discussion of law and religion in the American legal system begins with the text of the First Amendment. Divided into the Establishment Clause and the Free Exercise Clause, these sixteen words provide two distinct types of protection for religion. By restricting the role of organized religion in the federal system, the Establishment Clause prevents any single religion from controlling the national government. By extension, the Establishment Clause also protects all forms of organized religion from governmental interference.[1] In contrast, the Free Exercise Clause protects the rights of the individual, not just to hold religious beliefs, but to act on them without governmental interference. This protection for both group and individual religious activities is a uniquely American contribution, though based on hundreds of years of European history and the practical needs of a diverse young country.

Neither the Establishment Clause nor the Free Exercise Clause has an obvious application to land use and planning decisions. In fact, the majority of Establishment Clause cases over the past seventy-five years have involved public education, while most Free Exercise Clause cases have involved penalties for disfavored personal conduct. To date, the Supreme Court has addressed federal land use decisions directly in only one Free Exercise case.[2] However, as communities become ever more religiously diverse and land use conflicts heighten, local planning decisions are increasingly being seen through a religious prism. Where the First Amendment was originally intended to protect religious diversity at the national level, it is now being applied to decisions that implicate questions of diversity at the level of the local neighborhood.

For planners, the primary question under the Religion Clauses of the First Amendment is whether they are required, or allowed, to consider the effect of their decisions on religious interests. On a theoretical level, planning does not distinguish between religious and secular uses in siting or other land use decisions. The fact that a decision may burden an applicant's religious, instead of commercial, interests is not a physical planning concern, though it may be a political one. The difference between allowing local governments to factor religious interests into their decisions and compelling them to do so is frequently the difference between restricting and expanding religious diversity.

Understanding the history of the First Amendment is therefore essential to applying it to local planning decisions. First at the federal level, and then as it was expanded to the state and local governments, the First Amendment forced decision makers to consider the impact of their decisions on individual religious interests. While the Supreme Court has recently retreated from its activist role in First Amendment Religion Clause jurisprudence, planners are not free to ignore the consequences of land use decisions on religious freedom. The Court also made it clear that local governments have discretion to consider religious differences in their decision making if they so choose, provided they do not discriminate as a result.[3]

The Bill of Rights

There was never any question that personal religious beliefs or "rights of conscience" were to be protected in the young American republic. By the time of the Constitutional Convention, there was general agreement that matters of religious belief were outside the coercive power of government. Every state guaranteed liberty of conscience to its citizens through state constitutions and laws.[4] The only question for the delegates at the Constitutional Convention was what role the federal government would play in protecting religious liberty. The original answer was none. The final version of the Constitution did not contain a single mention of freedom of religion.[5] In fact, the document did not mention God, and it permitted the president to take office by oath or affirmation, at his choice. The only mention of religion was a strict prohibition on religious tests for any federal office or public trust added at the very end of Article VI, the last substantive section of the Constitution.[6] When asked why the Constitution did not refer to God, Alexander Hamilton supposedly responded that the nation did not need "foreign aid," or alternatively, "we forgot."[7]

A bill of rights, including guarantees of religious freedom, was the price of constitutional ratification exacted by the crucial states of Massachusetts, New York, and Virginia. Proposals for amendments to the Constitution came from every state ratifying convention.[8] James Madison spent months reviewing more than two hundred proposed amendments, eventually reducing them to seventeen. The House of Representatives adopted Madison's recommendations, with some modification. The Senate responded by combining and cutting them to twelve, with freedom of religion as the third item.[9] Washington sent the resulting twelve amendments to the states in October 1789. The first two were never ratified, leaving freedom of religion in the First Amendment by default.[10]

In its final form, the First Amendment prohibited two types of government action. First, it required the federal government to eschew any attempt to establish a national religion, like the Anglican Church in England, through official recognition or funding. Second, it assured individuals in broad terms that they could practice their religion without government interference. The details would be worked out later, through the next two hundred years of American history. Meanwhile, there was remarkable consensus among those early Americans that the government should stay out of the private sphere of personal belief and religion.[11]

That consensus, which blossomed in late 1791, was not easy to achieve. Members of the first Congress would have been intimately familiar with the history of religious strife in Europe over the preceding generations. England, the mother country for most Americans, had been wracked by religious conflict only a century earlier. France, Germany, Ireland, and Holland had their own histories of religious wars during the same period. In many ways, the First Amendment was the culmination of more than 150 years of experience brought by immigrants to the fledging republic.

The familiar myth taught to generations of American schoolchildren was that the first settlers came to the New World for religious freedom and toleration. The truth was far different. The early New England colonies adopted legal codes based on strict interpretation of the Old Testament, including the death penalty for "idolatry."[12] With the notable exceptions of Pennsylvania and Rhode Island, they levied taxes for the support of established churches, required adherence to church doctrine, deported or arrested dissenters, mandated church attendance, and required licenses to conduct services. Baptists and evangelical Christians were specially targeted for punishment throughout the colonies.[13]

The language of toleration and the reality of religious discrimination coexisted in colonial America. All of the southern colonies adopted the Church of England as their state religion.[14] The New England colonies provided free land and public funding for Protestant sects. In Maryland, only "Trinitarian Christians" were protected by the Religious Toleration Act of 1649.[15] During the same time period, Roger Williams and Anne Hutchinson were banished from Massachusetts Colony by the Puritan establishment. A century later, in 1774, the Anglican establishment in Virginia imprisoned dissenters who failed to obtain licenses before preaching to their followers.[16] In 1788, New York passed a law requiring public officials to renounce foreign authorities "in all matters ecclesiastical as well as civil," which was directly aimed at American Catholics.[17]

At virtually the same time it was imprisoning itinerant preachers, Virginia adopted its much admired 1776 Declaration of Rights, which announced in ringing terms:

> That religion, or the duty which we owe to our Creator, and the manner of discharging it, can be directed only by reason and conviction, not by force or violence; and therefore, all men are equally entitled to the free exercise of religion, according to the dictates of conscience, and that it is the mutual duty of all to practice Christian forbearance, love, and charity, towards each other.

With these quintessentially Lockean phrases reflecting the European Enlightenment in every syllable, the Virginia legislature moved freedom of religion from being bestowed by legislative grace to being an inalienable right available to all.[18] The Virginia legislature's affirmation that religious belief was beyond its power to control was an extraordinary moment in the history of religious liberty.

A far more contentious issue than freedom of religious belief was addressed by the Virginia legislature a decade later: whether the state should provide financial support to organized religion. Until the American Revolution, Virginia routinely funded Anglican churches; the practice was suspended during the war and was never officially reinstated. To formally end what he saw as a pernicious practice, Thomas Jefferson had drafted a statute prohibiting government support for recognized churches in 1777. It lay dormant until 1784, when a religious group requested public funding for its activities. With Jefferson in France on public business, James Madison responded in 1785 with his famed *Memorial and Remonstrance Against Religious Assessments*: "Who does not see that the same authority which can establish Christianity, in exclusion of all other Religions, may establish with the same ease any particular sect of Christians, in exclusion of all other Sects?" Though the battle was hard fought, the Virginia Statute for Religious Freedom, another milestone in the history of religious liberty, was adopted in 1786.[19]

Even before adoption of the First Amendment, the Congress of the Confederation followed the lead of Virginia and the other states with adoption of the Northwest Ordinance in 1787, providing that: "No person demeaning himself in a peaceable and orderly manner shall ever be molested on account of his mode of worship or religious sentiments in the said territory."[20] Eventually, the Northwest Territory was divided into the states of Ohio, Illinois, Indiana, Wisconsin, and Michigan, each with a federally mandated tradition of religious freedom.

Although the Enlightenment influence was considerable, religious freedom was a simple necessity for the young republic. For the most part, the individual states were religiously homogenous, with a clear majority professing a single faith. In contrast, the nation as a whole was much more religiously diverse, with no dominant religion. If for no other reason, a successful political union required that Quakers in Pennsylvania, Catholics in Maryland, Anglicans in Virginia, and Congregationalists in New England respect the others' religious faiths.[21] While the dominant state religions had a strong incentive for favoring an official national policy of tolerance, the minority religions, such as Baptists and Presbyterians, welcomed independence as an opportunity to escape the despised taxes levied to support established churches.[22] For different reasons, all of these groups saw the advantages of an official policy of nonestablishment and religious freedom.[23]

The commitment to protecting religious diversity in the interest of a national government could be seen in George Washington's famous correspondence with the Hebrew Congregation of Newport, Rhode Island, in 1790. In response to a letter from the Congregation, Washington expressed the idea that religious freedom was essential to the new government:

> It is now no more that toleration is spoken of, as if it was by the indulgence of one class of people, that another enjoyed the exercise of their inherent natural rights. For, happily, the Government of the United States, which gives to bigotry no sanction, to persecution no assistance, requires only that they who live under its protection, should demean themselves as good citizens . . . .[24]

In 1802, Thomas Jefferson famously described the Religion Clauses of the First Amendment as an "act of the whole American people . . . building a wall of separation between Church and State."[25] This description came in his reply to a letter from the members of the Danbury Baptist Association who complained that the state of Connecticut granted them only religious "favors" and not "rights" as a minority religion. This exchange was held against the long history of state laws in Massachusetts and Connecticut requiring dissenters to apply formally for an exemption from payment of state taxes for the support of established Congregationalist churches.[26]

From its inception, the First Amendment was remarkably effective in preventing the federal government from legislating religious conduct or belief. The states were slower to erase the last vestiges of colonial practices. In 1808, North Carolina refused to seat a Jew elected to the state legislature under a statute requiring elected officials to be Protestants. By 1840, Jews were entitled to full political equality in twenty-one of the nation's twenty-six states.[27] By the 1820s, every state except one had ceased collecting taxes for the support of religious institutions.[28] Massachusetts continued to pay Protestant ministers with tax money until 1833, although it allowed taxpayers to select the denomination and church with the sometimes grudging approval of a board of selectmen.[29]

New Religion Clause issues continued to arise at state and local levels throughout the nineteenth century, frequently entwined with national ambivalence about the flood of immigration. During the 1830s, the Pennsylvania legislature mandated daily Bible reading in the public schools. In 1844, four days of rioting erupted in Philadelphia after the school board granted Catholic students the right to read from the Catholic Douay translation of the Bible instead of the Protestant King James version. Thirteen people were killed and two Irish Catholic churches and a convent were destroyed in what became known as the Philadelphia Bible Riots, while public authorities stood by.[30] Laws regulating Bible reading in public schools, restricting public funding for parochial schools, requiring Sunday closings, and establishing Christianity as the national religion were all proposed at the state and national level over the next decades with varying degrees of success and controversy.[31]

The Constitution bound the thirteen colonies together in a political union; the First Amendment made it possible for the colonies to cede their political independence without compromising their independent religious identities. The ideological commitment to religious liberty represented by the First Amendment served the nation well as religious diversity increased in the individual states during successive waves of immigration. Nonetheless, the tensions of the nineteenth century set the stage for the legal battles over the First Amendment that arose after World War I.

The Religion Clauses

The Founders saw the Establishment and Free Exercise Clauses as serving distinctly different purposes, although both limit government power. The Establishment Clause is a limitation on government power to act affirmatively—that is, to force individual action. The Free Exercise Clause limits government authority to act negatively—that is, to prevent individuals from worshipping as they please. Both are essential to a free society.

The Free Exercise Clause protects the right to hold certain religious beliefs and to act on them according to the dictates of conscience. The founders were all familiar with John Locke's appeal to natural law in his *Letter Concerning Toleration*, first published in 1689. Locke argued that "liberty of conscience is every man's natural right, equally belonging to dissenters as to themselves; and that nobody ought to be compelled in matters of religion either by law or force." By defining religious freedom as a natural right, Locke placed it beyond the power of government to regulate.

Liberty of conscience was enshrined as an inalienable right in every state constitution.[32] As already discussed, the landmark Virginia Declaration of Rights described the free exercise of religion as outside the power of the state to deny. To the founders, free exercise included both the right to believe freely and to implement those beliefs through worship. The scope of worship was left to the individual, although it is likely that the founders expected most worship to consist of some form of organized prayer. The Free Exercise Clause, therefore, paralleled existing state protections for individual rights.

The Establishment Clause protects against forced support of religious institutions contrary to one's beliefs.[33] This concept was not adopted as early as the right to free exercise by the natural rights movement. The Declaration of Independence did not object to Britain's establishment of the Anglican Church, with the king as its head. It was not included in the Virginia Declaration of 1776, although it was added a decade later when the Virginia Statute for Religious Freedom was adopted in 1786. Most states, especially in the northeast, continued to collect taxes to support religious institutions for several decades. When adopted, the Establishment Clause overlaid a patchwork of state legislation concerning government endorsement of particular religious beliefs, either through funding or other action.

Evolution of Supreme Court Jurisprudence

Supreme Court jurisprudence in this area is effectively less than seventy-five years old. For more than 150 years, the Supreme Court held that the protections of the First Amendment did not apply to the states. After all, "congress" meant the national legislature.[34] In the 1873 *Slaughterhouse Cases*, the Court affirmed its position that federal protection of individual rights did not extend to state laws, despite passage of the Fourteenth Amendment.[35]

Beginning in 1925, the Supreme Court abruptly reversed course and incrementally began to restrict state power under the First Amendment. In *Gitlow v. New York*, the Court held that "freedom of speech and of the press—which are protected by the First Amendment from abridgment by Congress—are among the fundamental personal rights and 'liberties' protected by the due process clause of the Fourteenth Amendment from impairment by the state."[36] Although it was fundamentally a free speech case, *Gitlow* opened the door to application of other freedoms guaranteed to the states by the Bill of Rights.

In 1940, the Supreme Court held that the Free Exercise Clause applied to the states through the Fourteenth Amendment. In *Cantwell v. Connecticut*,[37] the state required all religious and charitable solicitation to be approved by a public official, who had the power to decide whether they were for bona fide purposes. The petitioners were three Jehovah's Witnesses arrested for door-to-door canvassing in violation of the law.[38] In a unanimous decision, the Supreme Court ruled that giving a state authority to decide what is a religious purpose unconstitutionally burdened the exercise of liberty protected by the Fourteenth Amendment. In addition to setting aside the convictions for fraudulent solicitation, the Court overturned a related conviction for breach of the peace, holding that it violated the free speech guarantees of the First Amendment, newly applicable to the states through the Fourteenth.

In 1947, the Supreme Court formally added the Establishment Clause to the list of individual rights applicable to the states through the Fourteenth Amendment.[39] In *Everson v. Board of Education of Ewing Township*, the Court gave an erudite history of the First Amendment, culminating in a holding that the Establishment Clause "requires the state to be a neutral in its relations with groups of religious believers and nonbelievers."[40] The five-member majority then applied its newly announced "neutrality" doctrine to uphold tax-funded payments to parents for bus transportation to both public and Catholic parochial schools. The dissent, written by Justice Jackson, lately returned from the Nuremberg trials, argued forcefully that transportation payments, although small, were a first step in the direction of establishment of religion, and impermissibly "entangled" the state in religious affairs.[41]

Because the Free Exercise Clause protects both belief and action, it frequently implicates other constitutional provisions, most notably the Free Speech Clause. The fraudulent solicitation charges in *Cantwell*, for instance, were decided under the Free Exercise Clause, while the breach of the peace claim was decided under Free Speech. The fact that Free Exercise rights are frequently expressed through speech became important in later Supreme Court jurisprudence, although it was not a focus in *Cantwell*. Presaging later Religion Clause cases, *Everson* looked at both the intent of the legislature in adopting the payment provisions, and the possible effect on the recipient's religious freedom.

It is not always easy to tell the difference between the Religion Clauses at the boundaries of Supreme Court jurisprudence. The Court itself often refers to the protections afforded by the First Amendment in general, without distinguishing between the Establishment and Free Exercise Clauses.[42] The two clauses may even conflict in practice, with overly solicitous religion-specific exemptions from generally applicable rules under the Free Exercise Clause potentially violating the prohibition on religious preference under the Establishment Clause.[43]

The Establishment Clause

The Establishment Clause is invoked when legislative actions appear to favor or disfavor particular religions, or religion in general. According to the Supreme Court, the Establishment Clause was intended to afford protection against three main evils: "[state] sponsorship, financial support, and active involvement" in religious affairs.[44] The *Everson* decision announced the overarching "neutrality" principle that is still applicable to both Religion Clauses. Since that time, the Supreme Court has tried a number of formulas in addition to neutrality to decide Establishment Clause cases, but has been unable to settle permanently on a single test.

In a series of cases after *Everson*, the Supreme Court developed a two-part test for Establishment Clause cases. First, does the statute have a secular legislative purpose? Second, does its primary effect either advance or inhibit religion?[45] The Court added a third part to the test in 1970 prohibiting "an excessive government entanglement with religion," reflecting the issue raised by Justice Jackson in his dissent to *Everson*.[46] In *Lemon v. Kutzman*, the three-part test was applied by Justice Burger to strike down multiple laws that allowed payment for secular teaching in parochial schools on entanglement grounds. As the Court grew more conservative during the 1980s and 1990s, it tested different formulations of the test in a series of 5–4 decisions, from the "endorsement" test proposed by Justice O'Connor[47] to the "coercion" test outlined by Justice Kennedy.[48] In *Agostini v. Felton*, another 5–4 decision in 1997, the Court returned to a two-part test, with excessive entanglement as a form of prohibited "effect" instead of an independent prong.[49]

The Court's disarray on Establishment Clause jurisprudence culminated in a pair of decisions. One allowed the Ten Commandments to remain publicly displayed at the Texas statehouse, and the other forbade the posting of the Ten Commandments on the walls of two Kentucky county courthouses. In *McCreary County v. American Civil Liberties Union of Kentucky*, the five-member majority examined the history of the county's decision to post the Ten Commandments and other documents with religious themes. Based on the facts, Justice Souter applied *Lemon*'s purpose test to strike down the public display for its "unmistakable" religious objective, despite the inclusion of other historical documents.[50] In his dissent, Justice Scalia reiterated his consistent criticism of *Lemon*, arguing that the Establishment Clause forbids only affirmative aid to particular religions, not support for religious belief in general.[51] Decided on the same day, *Van Orden v. Perry* allowed display of the Ten Commandments on a large stone monument donated to the state by a private fraternal group in 1961. The four-member plurality opinion, authored by Chief Justice Rehnquist, acknowledged that the display had a religious message, but concluded that it also represented the state's political and legal history. Despite the mixed religious and secular purpose, the plurality opined that the "passive display" did not convey intent to endorse religion.[52] The four-member dissent, written by Justice Stevens, reached the opposite conclusion about the primarily religious purpose of the monument.[53]

Justice Breyer cast the deciding votes in both *McCreary* and *Van Orden*, using a fact-based inquiry into the purpose of the display. In *McCreary*, he joined the majority's opinion that the history of the county's action showed a clear intent to endorse the religious message of the Ten Commandments. In *Van Orden*, he focused on the fact that the granite tablets were located in a large park containing a total of seventeen monuments and twenty-one historical markers with significance in Texas history. Breyer found that, viewed in context, the display communicated a predominantly moral and secular message allowed under the Establishment Clause.[54]

Although land use and planning decisions can implicate the Establishment Clause, it has generally not been a fruitful avenue of challenge. Following the Supreme Court's lead,[55] federal and state courts have upheld exemptions for religious uses from otherwise applicable zoning and land use requirements under the Establishment Clause. Applying a standard of "benevolent neutrality" and "permissible accommodation," the majorities in these courts view religiously based exemptions as a way of avoiding entanglement with religion rather than as impermissible favoritism.[56]

At the same time, the courts also find no obligation on the part of government to grant exemptions or adopt special rules for religious uses. Without serious analysis, the Supreme Court has simply assumed that land use regulations of general applicability are inherently "neutral" for the purposes of the Religion Clauses. In *Lemon*, Chief Justice Burger pointed to land regulations as especially unlikely to raise entanglement issues: "Fire inspections, building, and zoning regulations . . . are examples of necessary and permissible contacts."[57] Justice Rehnquist has similarly cited fire and safety regulations as state administrative regulations properly imposed on sectarian institutions.[58] Thus, unless a community is foolish enough to set aside public land for a specific denomination or to enter into an exclusive contract with a favored religious group, it is generally free to treat religious uses like any other use or to grant blanket exemptions from land use regulations without violating the Establishment Clause.

The Free Exercise Clause

The Free Exercise Clause is another matter. It is implicated when government action threatens to burden an individual's religious beliefs, either by preventing or penalizing those beliefs. More directly than the Establishment Clause, the Free Exercise Clause protects the individual, not organized religion. The Supreme Court's jurisprudence in this area has been even more checkered than under the Establishment Clause, responding both to national politics and the changing composition of the Court. As the Court protections for individual rights in general have ebbed and flowed, so has its Free Exercise jurisprudence.

Cantwell was just the beginning. It was followed less than two weeks later by *Minersville School District v. Gobitis*.[59] World War II, already raging in Europe, cast its shadow on every line of *Gobitis*. The two Gobitis children, both Jehovah's Witnesses, were expelled from their public school for refusing to salute the flag, as required by local regulation. Eight of the nine justices agreed that national unity and security considerations, exemplified in the salute, trumped individual free exercise rights when applied in a neutral manner. As later explained by Justice Frankfurter, the First Amendment granted freedom of belief, not freedom from acting in compliance with generally applicable laws because of that belief.

Only three years later, at the height of America's involvement in World War II, the Supreme Court reversed itself. In *West Virginia State Board of Education v. Barnette*,[60] decided in 1943, a six-member majority held that the children of Jehovah's Witnesses could not be compelled to salute the flag under threat of expulsion and potential prosecution for delinquency. According to the majority opinion: "The very purpose of a Bill of Rights was . . . to place [certain subjects] beyond the reach of majorities and officials and to establish them as legal principles to be applied by the courts."[61] Importing a test generally applicable to free speech cases, the Court held that the free exercise of religion authorized restriction "only to prevent grave and immediate danger" to the state.[62] Again foreshadowing future jurisprudential debates, Justice Frankfurter's dissent pointed to numerous instances where general law prevailed over personal religious scruples, including compulsory vaccination, food inspection, military service, testimonial oaths, and involuntary medical treatment.[63] He also warned against allowing courts to define the scope of "religion" under the First Amendment.[64]

In another Jehovah's Witness case, decided the following year, the Supreme Court upheld a misdemeanor conviction of nine-year-old Betty Prince's guardian, who had allowed the girl to sell religious tracts on a public street in violation of child labor laws.[65] Refusing to address whether the girl was actually selling religious materials, the Court concluded that the state's interest in regulating child labor outweighed the parent's admitted interest in free exercise and due process.[66] The dissent saw no reason to parse the Free Exercise Clause based on the age of the actor and no reason to deprive the child of the right to exercise her religion.[67] The same year, in a case involving adults, the Court struck down convictions for mail fraud resulting from allegedly false religious fundraising, on the grounds that the truth of religious belief was not susceptible to legal determination under the Religion Clauses.[68]

In 1961 the Court struck down a Maryland law requiring that notaries profess a belief in God as a condition of office.[69] But that same year, the Court ruled that a Pennsylvania Sunday closing law did not violate the free exercise rights of an Orthodox Jewish retailer, Abraham Braunfeld, whose religion prohibited him from remaining open on Saturday. In a notably unsympathetic opinion authored by Justice Burger, a 6–3 majority held that the law had a neutral secular purpose of providing a uniform day of rest and "merely" made it more expensive for Braunfeld to exercise his faith.[70] In other words, the State was not obligated to avoid financially burdening religious adherents, only to refrain from direct burdens on religious beliefs.

Finally, in 1963, the Supreme Court articulated a strict balancing test for violation of the Free Exercise Clause. In *Sherbert v. Verner*, the state of South Carolina refused to grant unemployment compensation to Adell Sherbert because her Seventh Day Adventist beliefs prevented her from accepting work on Saturdays, although it gave full benefits to Sunday worshippers. In addition to the "neutrality" requirement applicable to both Religion Clauses, the Court looked at whether the purpose or effect of the regulation "is to impede the observance of one or all religions, or is to discriminate invidiously between religions."[71] If so, the law presumptively violated the Free Exercise Clause even if it imposed only indirect burdens. Next, the Court asked whether there was a "compelling" state interest that justified infringing religious exercise. Where the Court had upheld burdens on free exercise, such as Sunday closings or child labor laws, it retrospectively found that the challenged conduct threatened public safety, peace, or order.[72] The Court found no state interest, much less a compelling one, in forcing Sherbert to choose between unemployment compensation and her religious beliefs.[73] In response to a spirited concurrence by Justice Stewart, the majority acknowledged that the decision could be construed as "establishment" of the Seventh Day Adventist religion, but then concluded that allowing unemployment benefits was no more than official neutrality in the face of religious diversity.[74]

In the twenty-five years after *Sherbert*, the Supreme Court decided a number of contentious Free Exercise or combination Religion Clause cases, with varying results. *Lemon v. Kutzman* has already been discussed. In *Wisconsin v. Yoder*, the Court refused to enforce a compulsory high school attendance law against Amish families. Although the statute was admittedly neutral, it interfered unnecessarily with the free exercise of the Amish parents' religion. The state failed to show a compelling interest in forcing Amish children to attend school beyond eighth grade, where the Amish demonstrated both a sincere religious belief and an adequate system of vocational education.[75] Based on these facts, the Court granted the Amish an express exemption from the generally applicable compulsory education statutes as an "accommodation" mandated by the neutrality doctrine.[76]

In *Thomas v. Review Board*, the Court struck down Indiana's denial of unemployment benefits to a Jehovah's Witness who quit his job after he was transferred to a new position fabricating weapons. The Indiana Supreme Court had found that his religious objections to war and armaments did not qualify as "good cause" for termination under state law. The Supreme Court ruled that the state's interpretation of "good cause" impermissibly burdened free exercise, albeit indirectly, because it resulted in substantial financial pressure on Mr. Thomas to violate his beliefs.[77] Without a compelling interest, which the Court did not find, the state was required to grant an exemption accommodating his beliefs. *Thomas* may have been the high point of the Court's solicitude for individual rights under the Free Exercise Clause.

In *United States v. Lee*, the Court upheld a federal requirement that Amish employers and employees must pay Social Security taxes, even though a statutory exemption was available to self-employed individuals. The Court had little difficulty finding the federal government had an overriding interest in maintaining the fiscal integrity of the Social Security system, sufficient to justify a burden on religious exercise.[78] Justice Stevens concurred with the result, but on the ground that the government should not be in "the business of evaluating the relative merits of differing religious claims" lest it violate the Establishment Clause. Harking back to *Everson*, Stevens proposed that valid and neutral laws of general applicability be presumed constitutional unless the individual demonstrated a unique reason for exemption. The entire burden, which Stevens described as "almost insurmountable," would be on the individual rather than the government.[79]

In the 1986 case *Goldman v. Weinberger*, an Orthodox Jew challenged the military's restrictions on headgear, which prevented him from wearing the skullcap mandated by his religion. In the interest of discipline and uniformity, the majority opinion deferred to military practice by upholding the regulation. The First Amendment did not require accommodation of individual religious beliefs where the government demonstrated a strong interest that was less than compelling for the military.[80] Justice Stevens again concurred on the ground that the regulation was neutral and completely objective, allowing for no exemptions.[81] The military's interest in a uniform dress code was less important to Stevens than the constitutional interest in "uniform treatment for the members of all religious faiths."[82] *Goldman* was one of a series of decisions in the mid-1980s that revealed deep divisions in the Justices' views of the Religion Clause. Five separate opinions came from the 5–4 decision, reflecting a turning point in Free Exercise jurisprudence.

In *Bowen v. Roy*, decided the same year as *Goldman*, parents challenged on religious grounds the requirement that they obtain a Social Security number for their child before receiving federal income assistance. Justice Burger, in a fairly dramatic retreat from his earlier decisions, upheld the rule as wholly neutral and uniform, without applying the heightened scrutiny mandated by *Sherbert* and *Lemon*. Perhaps influenced by the unconventional nature of the parents' beliefs, the majority decision opined that the federal government did not need to show a compelling state interest or least restrictive means where there was no government compulsion, no intent to discriminate, and the restraints were incidental to the reasonable needs of the program.[83] Justice O'Connor objected that the majority had set the Free Exercise bar so low as to be almost nonexistent. *Bowen* generated another five opinions, further muddling the Court's Free Exercise test.

In *Lyng v. Northwest Indian Cemetery Protective Association*, the Court rejected a Free Exercise challenge to federal construction of a road through the Chimney Rock section of the Six Rivers National Forest in California, an area traditionally held sacred by three Native American tribes. Citing *Bowen*, Justice O'Connor agreed that the road would virtually destroy the Indians' ability to practice their religion, but nonetheless limited the reach of the Free Exercise Clause to government programs that coerce individuals into acting contrary to their religious beliefs or discriminate against religions.[84] The majority opinion did not require the Forest Service to demonstrate any interest in the road construction, much less a compelling interest. In fact, where the effects on religion were incidental to otherwise lawful activities, the government had no obligation to consider the impact of its actions on religious exercise.[85] Though involving proprietary decisions by the federal government, *Lyng* is nonetheless the only Supreme Court decision addressing the relationship between land use and Free Exercise.

All of the Free Exercise cases decided in the quarter-century after *Sherbert* involved laws of neutral application with valid public purposes. It is not possible to explain the Court's informal abandonment of heightened scrutiny solely by reference to the facts of the cases themselves. In *Bowen*, the Court attempted to distinguish its earlier heightened scrutiny by explaining that it applied only in cases involving religious compulsion rather than those merely denying a government benefit.

Although the Court had been willing to compel affirmative acts (for example, compulsory vaccinations) in the interest of public health, the Court seems to have assumed that these requirements would have survived strict scrutiny and the compelling interest test. The dramatic change in the Court's Free Exercise Clause jurisprudence during the mid-1980s was part of a general change in its attitude toward government entitlements and individual rights. In the 1960s and 1970s, the Court saw the withholding of a government financial benefit as a form of economic coercion with individual religious consequences. By the mid-1980s, the Court no longer required the government to justify withholding a benefit, but instead required the individual to justify the entitlement by demonstrating compliance with governmental regulations.

All of these jurisprudential currents came together in 1990 in the Court's still controversial decision on *Employment Division v. Smith*.[86] Smith and his co-worker, Black, were fired from their jobs for ingesting peyote during Native American ceremonies. Their applications for unemployment insurance were denied because their terminations were based on consumption of a controlled substance, a felony under Oregon law. After lengthy proceedings, the Oregon Supreme Court ruled that the state statute violated the Free Exercise Clause because it made no exception for sacramental drug use. Under *Sherbert*, the Court had already held that the state did not have a compelling interest in enforcing its drug laws through the unemployment system.[87] Under these precedents, the state could not deny unemployment benefits on the basis of religiously motivated peyote use.

The U.S. Supreme Court reversed on every point, discarding fifty years of precedent and holding that neutral, generally applicable laws could not be challenged under the Free Exercise Clause. The Court stated that an individual's religious beliefs provided no excuse for ignoring an otherwise valid law. Citing *Reynolds*,[88] *Gobitis, Prince,* and *Braunfeld*, all decided before *Sherbert*, the majority adopted a "bright line" test for neutral laws, with no balancing of governmental and individual interests. The Court's new formulation asked only whether the regulation is nondiscriminatory and applies generally. The fact that the regulation burdens religious practice need not be considered. The "compelling interest" test in *Sherbert* was expressly rejected as administratively impractical. The distinction between coercive laws and those involving a governmental benefit was rejected. The government has no obligation to demonstrate a compelling or important interest in the law, nor must it show that the regulation is narrowly tailored to accomplish its purpose. Although the Court did not overrule its unemployment compensation precedents, it found them irrelevant to generally applicable criminal laws. Because Oregon's ban on peyote was neutral and generally applicable, the state was entitled both to punish the conduct directly and to deny unemployment benefits on the basis of its violation.

Smith caused a firestorm of protest from religious groups and in Congress. Although the Court expressly permitted nondiscriminatory religious practice exemptions from general laws, it left such accommodations strictly to the political process. The Court recognized that this result would undoubtedly disadvantage minority religions, but viewed this as simply an "unavoidable consequence of democratic government."[89] The result was particularly unpalatable to religious groups that had grown accustomed to seeking judicial relief when the political system failed to recognize and take account of impacts on individual religious practice, especially for members of minority religions. As discussed in later chapters, they sought a political remedy to the turmoil caused by the *Smith* decision.

Since *Smith*, far fewer Free Exercise cases wend their way through the federal system. Nonetheless, the Supreme Court has struck down one set of statutes in the intervening period. In *Church of the Lukumi Babalu Aye v. City of Hialeah*, the city adopted companion ordinances prohibiting the ritual sacrifice or slaughtering of animals within its limits but exempting animals intended as food, including kosher slaughter.[90] After a thorough examination of the history of the ordinances, the Court held that they were neither neutral nor generally applicable. Instead, the Court found that the ordinances were unmistakably aimed at the Santeria religion, in response to public concern about the opening of a church center in the city. Faced with a law adopted for discriminatory motives, which singled out a disfavored religion, the Court promptly reverted to the old "compelling interest" and "narrowly tailored" tests.[91] The Hialeah ordinances failed this revival of strict scrutiny.

Planners should not read too much into the Supreme Court's willingness to strike down ordinances intended to prevent particular religious practices, without an arguably neutral purpose. In its general First Amendment jurisprudence, the Court has been willing to allow much more public involvement in the religious sphere than would have seemed possible even twenty-five years ago.

Notes

1. The Establishment Clause "was intended not only to keep the states' hands out of religion, but to keep religion's hands off the state." *Everson v. Bd. of Educ. of Ewing Tp.*, 330 U.S. 1, 26–27 (1947) (Jackson, J., dissenting).
2. *Lyng v. Nw. Indian Cemetery Protective Assn.*, 485 U.S. 439 (1988).
3. *See, e.g., Employment Div. v. Smith*, 494 U.S. 872 (1990); *Lyng v. Nw. Indian Cemetery Protective Assn.*, 485 U.S. 439.
4. Noah Feldman, Divided By God 42 (paperback ed. 2006).
5. John Meacham, American Gospel 90 (paperback ed. 2007). Only one petition on religious freedom was submitted to the Constitutional Convention, by Jonas Phillips, a Jew.
6. The Declaration of Independence mentioned a supreme being four times, each time using a different formulation. The Articles of Confederation, adopted in 1781, did not reference God or religion at all.
7. Brooke Allen, *Our Godless Constitution*, The Nation, Feb. 21, 2005.
8. The Bill of Rights: Original Meaning and Current Understanding 3 (E. Hickok, Jr. ed. 1991).

9. Peter Irons, God on Trial: Dispatches from America's Religious Battlefields 14 (2007).
10. Frank Donovan, Mr. Madison's Constitution 120 (1965).
11. Meacham, *supra* note 5, at 19.
12. Irons, *supra* note 9, at 3–4; Meacham, *supra* note 5, at 53.
13. Irons, *supra* note 9, at 5–7.
14. Feldman, *supra* note 4, at 31.
15. Meacham, *supra* note 5, at 52.
16. *Id.* at 68.
17. Irons, *supra* note 9, at 20.
18. Meacham, *supra* note 5, at 69, quoting from William Lee Miller, The First Liberty: American Foundation in Religious Freedom (exp. ed., Georgetown University Press 2003) (1986).
19. Meacham, *supra* note 5, at 85–86. Near the end of his life, Thomas Jefferson showed the importance he gave to the principles of the Establishment Clause when he wrote the text of his own epitaph: *Here was buried Thomas Jefferson author of the Declaration of American Independence, of the Statute of Virginia for Religious Freedom, and Father of the University of Virginia.*
20. Meacham, *supra* note 5, at 90.
21. Feldman, *supra* note 4, at 44.
22. *Id.* at 33.
23. *Id.* at 25.
24. Meacham, *supra* note 5, at 261.
25. The "wall of separation" metaphor was earlier used by Roger Williams and Isaac Backus, a New England Baptist. Feldman, *supra* note 4, at 24, 256.
26. *Id.* at 33.
27. Meacham, *supra* note 5, at 107–08.
28. *See Everson*, 333 U.S. at 10–11.
29. Meacham, *supra* note 5, at 82.
30. Irons, *supra* note 9, at 20–21.
31. *See, e.g., Bd. of Educ. of Cincinnati v. Minor*, 23 Ohio St. 211, 13 Am. Rep. 233 (1872) (upholding a resolution adopted by the local school board prohibiting religious instruction and Bible reading in the public schools).
32. Feldman, *supra* note 4, at 42.
33. In his *Letter Concerning Toleration*, John Locke also argued that it is "necessary to distinguish exactly the business of civil

government from that of religion and to settle the just bounds that lie between the one and the other."

34. *Barron v. Baltimore*, 32 U.S. 243 (1833).
35. 83 U.S. 36 (1873).
36. 268 U.S. 652, 666 (1925).
37. 310 U.S. 296 (1940).
38. Jehovah's Witnesses took forty-five cases to the Supreme Court in the seventeen-year period between 1938 and 1955 in an organized campaign to establish and define the scope of First Amendment protections. They won thirty-six of the cases. IRONS, *supra* note 9, at 19.
39. Alone among the current members of the Supreme Court, Justice Thomas continues to reject incorporation of the Establishment Clause into the Fourteenth Amendment. He argues that states retain their original freedom to establish religion.
40. *Everson,* 330 U.S. at 18.
41. *Id.* at 58.
42. *See, e.g., Lemon v. Kurtzman*, 403 U.S. 602, 612 (1971), and *Wisconsin v. Yoder*, 406 U.S. 205, 219 (1972).
43. *Wallace v. Jaffree*, 472 U.S. 38, 82–83 (1985) (O'Connor, J., concurring).
44. *Lemon v. Kurtzman*, 403 U.S. at 612.
45. *Bd. of Educ. v. Allen*, 392 U.S. 236, 243 (1968).
46. *Walz v. Tax Comm'n*, 397 U.S. 664, 674 (1970).
47. *Lynch v. Donnelly*, 465 U.S. 668 (1984) (O'Connor, J., concurring).
48. *Allegheny County v. ACLU*, 492 U.S. 573 (1989) (Kennedy, J., dissenting).
49. 521 U.S. 203 (1997).
50. *McCreary County v. ACLU*, 545 U.S. 844, 883 (2005).
51. *Id.* at 885 (Scalia, J., dissenting).
52. *Van Orden v. Perry*, 545 U.S. 677, 681 (2005) (Rehnquist, J., plurality opinion).
53. *Id.* at 707 (Stevens, J., dissenting).
54. *Id.* at 698 (Breyer, J., concurring).
55. *Corp. of the Presiding Bishop of the Church of Jesus Christ of Latter-Day Saints v. Amos*, 483 U.S. 327, 338 (1987); *Mueller v. Allen*, 463 U.S. 388, 393 (1983).

56. These cases frequently result in split decisions. *See, e.g., Ehlers-Renzi v. Connelly Sch. of the Holy Child, Inc.*, 224 F.3d 283 (4th Cir. 2000) (2–1 decision), *cert. denied*, 531 U.S. 1192 (2001); *Boyajian v. Gatzunis*, 212 F.3d 1 (1st Cir. 2000) (2–1 decision), *cert. denied*, 531 U.S. 1070 (2001); *Cohen v. City of Des Plaines*, 8 F.3d 484 (7th Cir. 1993); *East Bay Asian Local Dev. Corp. v. Cal.*, 24 Cal. 4th 693 (2000).
57. *Lemon v. Kurtzman*, 403 U.S. at 614.
58. *Wallace v. Jaffree*, 472 U.S. at 82–83 (Rehnquist, J., dissenting).
59. *Minersville Sch. Dist. v. Gobitis*, 310 U.S. 586 (1940).
60. *W. Va. St. Bd. of Educ. v. Barnette*, 319 U.S. 624, 653 (1943) (Frankfurter, J., dissenting).
61. *Id.* at 637, 653.
62. *Id.* at 640, 653.
63. *Id.* at 654 (Frankfurter, J., dissenting).
64. *Id.* at 658 (Frankfurter, J., dissenting).
65. *Prince v. Mass.*, 321 U.S. 158 (1944).
66. *Id.* at 164.
67. *Id.* at 171.
68. *United States v. Ballard*, 322 U.S. 78 (1944).
69. *Torcaso v. Watkins*, 367 U.S. 488 (1961).
70. *Braunfeld v. Brown*, 366 U.S. 599 (1969).
71. 374 U.S. 398, 404 (1963).
72. *Id.* at 403.
73. Even if the state had been able to show a paramount interest in the regulation, the Court suggested it would have had to demonstrate that "no alternative forms" were acceptable to achieve the same ends without burdening constitutional rights. *Id.* at 407.
74. *Id.* at 409.
75. 406 U.S. 205, 235 (1972).
76. *Id.* at 235 n.22.
77. 450 U.S. 707, 717 (1981).
78. 455 U.S. 252, 259 (1982).
79. *Id.* at 262–63 n.3.
80. 475 U.S. 503 (1986).
81. *Id.* at 514.

82. *Id.* at 512.
83. 476 U.S. 693 (1986).
84. 485 U.S. 439 (1983).
85. *Id.* at 451.
86. 494 U.S. 872 (1990).
87. 301 Or. 209, 217–19, 721 P.2d 445, 449–50 (1986), *vacated*, 485 U.S. 660, 674 (1988), *on remand*, 307 Or. 68, 72–73, 763 P.2d 146, 147–48 (1988), *reversed*, 494 U.S. 872 (1990).
88. *Reynolds v. United States*, 98 U.S. 145 (1878). In *Reynolds*, the Supreme Court held that criminal laws punishing polygamy could be enforced against Mormons without violating the Free Exercise Clause.
89. *Employment Div. v. Smith*, 494 U.S. at 890.
90. 508 U.S. 520 (1993).
91. *Id.* at 546.

The History of RLUIPA[1]

2

Marci A. Hamilton

RLUIPA is the quintessential legislative product—it is a compromise bill, stripped of elements in earlier drafts and containing oddly paired issues: land use and institutionalized persons involving religious individuals and institutions. RLUIPA could aptly be described as "sausage." One cannot understand RLUIPA without also knowing what happened with its precursors, the Religious Freedom Restoration Act of 1993 and the Religious Liberty Protection Act bills.[2]

RLUIPA's Predecessor: The Religious Freedom Restoration Act

The Religious Freedom Restoration Act (RFRA) was enacted to "correct" the Supreme Court's free exercise decision in *Employment Division v. Smith*, in which two drug counselors who used peyote during a Native American Church service were fired for using an illegal drug.[3] The case addressed whether a religious justification could be used to avoid Oregon's workmen's compensation and drug laws. The Court held the Free Exercise Clause did not mandate state accommodation, and, therefore, the drug counselors were subject to the state's neutral, generally applicable laws.

Before *Smith*, a handful of cases had applied strict scrutiny to unemployment compensation cases and to Wisconsin's compulsory education laws.[4] But, as the Court stated in *Smith*, the "vast majority" of its cases have upheld the "government's ability to enforce generally applicable prohibitions of socially harmful conduct."[5] The Court quoted its earlier decision in *Gillette v. United States*, where Justice Marshall, on behalf of the majority, explained: "Our cases do not at their farthest reach support the proposition that a stance of conscientious opposition relieves an objector from any colliding duty fixed by a democratic government."[6]

The Court further explained that although accommodation was not mandatory, it may be permissible for a state legislature to enact an accommodation by creating an exception to a law for religious practices. The Court's example was directly on point: the opinion highlighted state laws that had already exempted the religious use of peyote from their laws. Thus, the primary message of *Smith* was that neutral, generally applicable laws apply to everyone, regardless of belief, but elected bodies could carve out exceptions in circumstances thought to be appropriate.[7] Finally, discrimination based on religion would continue to be subject to strict scrutiny.

Despite the many cases in tension with their view, religious entities before *Smith* argued their cases as though strict scrutiny was the sole governing standard and that religious accommodation was mandatory under the Free Exercise Clause. When *Smith* explicitly rejected strict scrutiny in favor of rational review of neutral, generally applicable laws, religious lobbyists reacted strongly, turning away from the court toward the political process.

Following *Smith*, religious and civil rights groups prevailed upon Congress to expand religious liberty and civil rights guarantees beyond the Court's interpretation of the Constitution in *Smith*. They proposed that the strict scrutiny standard in a handful of cases preceding *Smith* and involving the unemployment context should be extended across all laws. Congress eagerly acquiesced and enacted RFRA, which instituted strict scrutiny of every law in the country that was found to substantially burden a religious individual or institution. It was invalidated less than four years later in *City of Boerne v. Flores*.[8]

Boerne (pronounced "bur-nee") addressed the question whether a church seeking demolition of its building was subject to the city's historical preservation laws. As soon as RFRA was passed, the church invoked it to avoid such laws. The Court never got to the merits because it addressed the city's facial, constitutional challenge to RFRA, and struck down the statute. According to the Court, RFRA and its legislative history challenged the Court's authority to interpret the First Amendment in violation of the separation of powers, trenched on every state law in direct repudiation of the inherent limits of federalism, and attempted to wring a constitutional amendment outside the mandatory Article V procedures from a statutory enactment.[9]

The Court reasoned that RFRA violated the inherent limits of federalism by forcing the states to do more than the Constitution required, in a situation where there was little or no proof that the states were engaging in unconstitutional conduct. The Court devised the standard still in use today: Congress may "enforce" the constitutional guarantees of the Fourteenth Amendment against the states by forcing states to go beyond constitutional requirements only if the law is congruent and proportional to the magnitude of the constitutional violations.[10] In the absence of general knowledge about, or a congressional record proving, widespread and persistent constitutional violations by the states, Congress was not at liberty to invalidate state action or laws. The Court held that there was no such supporting record behind RFRA.[11]

Even though RFRA's actual impact on the states would be enormous, the overwhelming focus of the hearings on RFRA was Supreme Court doctrine, as opposed to the policies of the states or even religious practices that might justify such an all-encompassing law. No less than 405 pages of legislative history were devoted to castigating the Court for its decision in *Smith*. Congress simply did not consider the policy ramifications that would follow the enactment of RFRA and that would make it harder for governments to enforce neutral, generally applicable laws.

As it turned out, RFRA meant that laws traditionally in the realm of the states, from family law (including adoption and medical neglect standards), to immunization exemptions, to land use law, would be altered through its application. Neither state nor local officials were called in to consult on its impact. Nor was there any effort by Congress to assess the potential impact of RFRA on the states or the federal government.

The Religious Liberty Protection Act Bills

After *City of Boerne v. Flores* invalidated RFRA, Congress introduced the Religious Liberty Protection Acts of 1998 and 1999 (RLPA), which attempted to reenact RFRA through Article I powers, specifically the Commerce and Spending Clauses.[12] Like its predecessor, RLPA would have introduced strict scrutiny for laws, including land use laws imposing a substantial burden on religious entities.

The hearings for RLPA on land use did not survey, examine, or even take into account the settled law of land use. No land use expert, either from the government or the universities, was asked to testify to explain either prevailing legal principles in the field or to analyze RLPA's potential impact on the law. Nor was there any attempt to investigate the existing principles applied to landowners and religious landowners in the land use process.

The same problem that was endemic to RFRA—an unimaginably large scope of application—infected deliberations over the never-enacted RLPA. Once again, the members of Congress did not ask the hard questions about the law that might have unveiled the law's unintended, but inevitable, consequences.

Both RFRA and RLPA attempted to institute strict scrutiny of a huge swath of laws. RFRA, which was intended to be an exercise of Congress's power under section 5 of the Fourteenth Amendment, applied to every law in the country. RLPA aimed for the same expanse, but would have done so through Congress's power under the Commerce and Spending Clauses, not just section 5 of the Fourteenth Amendment. The huge, although unspecified, scope of both acts, combined with their religiocentric titles, meant that it was difficult for sponsors to focus on any single application of the bills to existing laws. Hearings thus tended to be wide ranging, and unsupported generalizations were the norm, with no particular area of law receiving any degree of comprehensive treatment.

After it became clear that RLPA could not be passed—primarily as a result of lobbying by children's advocates, civil rights advocates concerned about fair housing laws, and conservative Christian organizations concerned about the principles of federalism—many believed that the momentum for a federal law that would impose strict scrutiny on all laws for the benefit of religious entities could not be revived. They were wrong, at least in part.

In response to persistent lobbying by conservative religious representatives, the American Civil Liberties Union (ACLU) and the Department of Justice drafted a land use/prison bill that was transformed in the hands of the ACLU into a land use/institutionalized persons bill. No hearings were held on this pared-down version of RLPA; rather, the prior hearings on RLPA generally addressing land use law (and prisons) were treated as hearings in support of the new RLUIPA bill,[13] and became the sole legislative history.

The Significance of the Legislative History and Record

The Court's decision in *Boerne v. Flores* invalidating RFRA shocked the members of Congress because for the first time in many decades the Court had refused to rubber stamp Congress's record. During the three years of Congress's consideration of RFRA, the members added hundreds of pages to the record excoriating the Supreme Court's interpretation of the Free Exercise Clause in *Employment Division v. Smith*, but very few pages were devoted to the object of their enactment: federal, state, and local laws, and those protected by such laws. They were enacting a law with enormous impact, affecting every law in the country, yet they put into the record only a small number of anecdotes regarding an even smaller number of laws affecting religious conduct. In response, the Court declined to presume that the states were engaged in widespread free exercise violations (particularly in the absence of any general knowledge of such violations), and refused to find the few anecdotes sufficient to show a pattern of unconstitutional conduct that would justify RFRA's sweeping impact on all state (and federal) laws.

Despite RFRA's enormous impact on state laws and governance, Congress did not introduce into the record any assessment of the law by state officials because it was unconcerned about such impact. Nor did Congress make any attempt to bring state or local governments into the three years of deliberation. At the last minute, Senator Reid attempted to create an exception for the prisons, but his objection was too late. The law's momentum was too strong, and RFRA was passed in 1993 without an exception through voice vote of the few members present in the House and by recorded vote in the Senate. (The House procedure is called "unanimous consent," hence the frequent and misleading claim by RFRA's supporters that it was passed "unanimously.") From the viewpoint of the members of Congress, RFRA was aimed toward the Supreme Court, with an incidental and constitutionally irrelevant effect on the states.

Boerne yanked Congress's attention away from its project of correcting the Supreme Court and back to its obligation to respect the separate sovereignty of the states. The *Boerne* decision instructed Congress to consider whether the states were, in fact, committing constitutional violations that justified serious federal intervention. Congress could not treat its powers as plenary, but rather as limited by state powers. This did not sit well. Immediately following *Boerne*, the House held hearings, this time venting its disapproval of *Boerne*.

RLPA was introduced against this backdrop. On the one hand, Congress was fuming over the Court's presumptuous recapture of power in *Boerne*, but on the other hand, if it wanted a bill affecting the states to pass constitutional muster, it had to at least appear to be in line with constitutional limitations. The RLPA hearings did improve upon RFRA's by more closely focusing on constitutionality.[14] Yet, there was no increased attention to state interests.

The hearings on RLPA covered several topics, including land use. Virtually all of those testifying, except me, supported the move to increase the power of religious landowners in the land use process. Under the Court's federalism jurisprudence, Congress had two paths open. Either the unconstitutional conduct of the states was so notorious (similar to the civil rights era) that all could agree without further proof that the states required federal correction burdening them with federal regulation exceeding constitutional requirements, or Congress needed to put together a record that showed a *widespread and recent pattern* of *unconstitutional* conduct in the states.

The RLPA legislative history regarding alleged land use abuses is short on examples of intentional discrimination against religious entities in the land use process and much heavier on complaints from religious entities about the burdens of ordinary land use laws and the lengthy time period for a typical land use application to go through the usual process. The House Report attempted to meet its burden of proving persistent and widespread unconstitutional discrimination through an adjective, summarizing this evidence as "massive."[15] Most of the courts that have considered the issue have relied on the adjective, rather than review of the actual legislative record.

The sparseness of the record concerning assertions of unconstitutional actions by land use authorities made in the RLPA hearings is on par with the inadequate record in *Boerne* on religious animus, and with the meager record of disability discrimination by the states during enactment of the ADA, the latter of which was held inadequate in *Board of Trustees of the University of Alabama v. Garrett*.[16] The inadequacy of the record in the land use context is emphasized when the handful of examples offered to show discrimination is considered against the backdrop of thousands of zoning authorities across the fifty states handling applications from many thousands of landowners. The sheer size of the land use universe makes the record of unconstitutional conduct cited in the RLPA hearings not "massive," but rather minute.

The First Amendment, before and after *Smith*, has prohibited discrimination on the basis of religion or religious belief. Therefore, lawsuits to redress discrimination could have been brought at any time, with or without RFRA, RLPA, or RLUIPA. Yet, the legislative history is bereft of cases showing intentional discrimination on the part of land use authorities. The legislative history also cites a study conducted by Brigham Young University, which presumes that safety and traffic issues in land use cases are a pretext for discrimination against "minority" churches, but provides no proof to support this presumption of discriminatory purpose.[17] Moreover, the study neither justifies its use of the term "minority" nor explains how it chose the instances it examines.

The Presbyterian Church conducted a survey of its congregation and generated a report regarding land use issues. According to this study, the Church won 67 percent of its land use challenges before 1980 and only 57 percent of its land use challenges after

1980. There was no explanation of why 1980 was chosen as a relevant dividing line, no disclosure of the total number of actual cases, and no indication that this uptick in losses was caused by unconstitutional government conduct. Nor was there any intimation that it was due to anti-Presbyterian bias in the land use process.

The vast majority of the evidence gathered by Congress in the RLPA hearings regarding land use authorities and churches involved garden variety land use laws. While such laws create "burdens" in the colloquial sense, the incidental burdens caused by such generally applicable laws are constitutional. During the RLPA hearings, church representatives criticized the following typical land use restrictions: (1) occupancy requirements, (2) limits on operational hours, (3) requirements to purchase adjacent residential lots in order to build church structures in residential zones, (4) the zoning approval process to convert a school to religious use, (5) landmarking laws, (6) distinctions drawn by land planners between tax-generating and tax-exempt properties, (7) zoning restrictions, and (8) the requirement that a religious landowner must own at least a leasehold on a property to have legal standing to challenge zoning regulations.

The RLPA testimony regarding land use also included references to certain editorial remarks of private individuals participating in the public hearings that are part and parcel of the land use process. Claims were made about anti-Semitic remarks, an anti-Pentecostal remark, and racially motivated remarks. Private prejudice, although distasteful and immoral, is not unconstitutional. United States citizens have the right to believe whatever they choose, free of government coercion, and the right to express unpopular views in open government forums. In order for the private prejudice described in the RLPA testimony to rise to the level of a constitutional violation, the government would have to embrace the prejudicial purpose. There was no indication in the RLPA testimony or record that the government in the circumstances described was motivated or controlled by unconstitutional discriminatory purpose.

Testimony that would have brought into question the broad and general claims about discrimination against "minority" religions was not permitted into the record. By the time RLUIPA was introduced, the most scientific study of land use data and churches to date was published in the *Journal of Church and State.*[18] Sociology professor Mark Chaves and William Tsitsos took their data from the 1998 National Congregations Study. The data indicated that only 1 percent of those religious institutions seeking a permit or license were denied. Moreover, of the six congregations that encountered problems in the zoning process, five were from mainstream religious groups, not minority religions as cited by the Brigham Young study in the RLPA testimony. The Chaves study was brought to the attention of the members of Congress, but Professor Chaves was not asked to testify, and the study itself was not included in the record.

Another point of view on land use available to Congress, but not included in the record, was a letter written by Mayor Rudolph Giuliani of New York City. With land use planning an important priority in large cities, he implored Congress to slow RLUIPA down and to permit the cities to become involved in the dialogue. His letter was not acted upon and not included or even mentioned in the record, and he was not invited to testify.

RLUIPA was introduced on July 13, 2000. Years earlier, when RLPA was pending, local government groups—including the National League of Cities and the National Association of Counties—organized an off-the-record briefing session for Congress. However, despite their persistent requests to testify at the RLUIPA hearings, they were never permitted to do so.

There were no hearings for objectors to express their views publicly, but opponents were informed before the summer recess of 2000 that RLUIPA would be revisited after the recess and their concerns would be heard. However, contrary to these assurances, House and Senate leadership successfully routed mounting opposition by passing RLUIPA by voice vote in both Chambers during the evening immediately preceding the summer recess. Most members were already headed back to their districts and had no idea the bill was on the agenda.

Conclusion

The road to the Religious Land Use and Institutionalized Persons Act begins with the Religious Freedom Restoration Act and then winds through the Religious Liberty Protection Act. It consists of two completely distinct areas of law that have been singled out for special attention—land use and prisons (or, in the larger sense, institutionalized persons). Both laws rest on an assertion that there was such widespread discrimination against religious entities that federal intervention into areas of traditional state prerogative must occur, though neither congressional record is particularly strong in its case for discrimination.

RLUIPA provides special privileges to religious entities in the land use process that are not available to any other landowners or developers. The Supreme Court has not yet taken up the question of the constitutionality of RLUIPA's land use provisions, although it upheld the prison provisions against an Establishment Clause attack in a case that explicitly set aside the land use provisions: *Cutter v. Wilkinson.*[19] In *Cutter,* Justice Thomas strongly hinted that he believed there might well be a reason to ask whether Congress held the power to enact RLUIPA.[20] This remains an open question.

Notes

1. This chapter is taken in large part from Marci A. Hamilton, *Federalism and the Public Good: The True Story Behind the Religious Land Use and Institutionalized Persons Act*, 78 Ind. L.J. 311 (2003).
2. *See* Religious Freedom Restoration Act of 1993, 42 U.S.C. § 2000bb (2001); Religious Liberty Protection Act of 1998, H.R. 4019, 105th Cong. (1998); Religious Liberty Protection Act of 1999, H.R. 1691, 106th Cong. (1999).
3. 494 U.S. 872 (1990).
4. *Sherbert v. Verner*, 374 U.S. 398 (1963) (unemployment compensation); *Wisconsin v. Yoder*, 406 U.S. 205 (1972) (compulsory education).
5. *Employment Div. v. Smith*, 494 U.S. 872 (1990).
6. 401 U.S. 437, 461 (1971).
7. For a more in-depth examination of permissive legislative accommodation, see Marci A. Hamilton, God vs. the Gavel: Religion and the Rule of Law (2005).
8. 521 U.S. 507 (1997). In the interest of full disclosure, I represented the City of Boerne, Texas, before the Supreme Court.

9. U.S. Const. art. V, which states:

    The Congress, whenever two thirds of both Houses shall deem it necessary, shall propose Amendments to this Constitution, or, on the Application of the Legislatures of two thirds of the several States, shall call a Convention for proposing Amendments, which, in either Case, shall be valid to all Intents and Purposes, as part of this Constitution, when ratified by the Legislatures of three fourths of the several States, or by Conventions in three fourths thereof, as the one or the other Mode of Ratification may be proposed by the Congress; Provided that no Amendment which may be made prior to the Year One thousand eight hundred and eight shall in any Manner affect the first and fourth Clauses in the Ninth Section of the first Article; and that no State, without its Consent, shall be deprived of its equal Suffrage in the Senate.

10. *City of Boerne v. Flores*, 521 U.S. at 519–20.
11. *Id.* at 530. A comparison between RFRA and the Voting Rights Act is instructive. In contrast to the record that confronted Congress and the Judiciary in the voting rights cases, RFRA's legislative record lacks examples of modern instances of generally applicable laws passed because of religious bigotry.
12. *See supra* note 2.
13. H.R. 4862, 106th Cong. (2000).
14. *See Issues Relating to Religious Liberty Protection, and Focusing on the Constitutionality of a Religious Protective Measure: Hearing Before the Senate Comm. on the Judiciary*, 106th Cong. (1999).
15. 146 Cong. Rec. S7774 (daily ed. July 27, 2000) (remarks of Sen. Hatch).
16. 531 U.S. 356 (2001).
17. *See, e.g., Religious Liberty Protection Act of 1998: Hearings on H.R. 4019 Before the Subcomm. on the Constitution of the House Comm. on the Judiciary*, 105th Cong. 131–53 (1998) (testimony of Prof. Cole W. Durham, Jr.). This study was conducted originally by the law firm of Mayer, Brown, and Platt.
18. Mark Chaves and William Tsitsos, *Are Congregations Constrained by Government? Empirical Results from the National Congregations Study*, 42 J. Church & St. 335 (2000).

19. 544 U.S. 709 (2005).
20. *Id.* at 727 n.2 (Thomas, J., concurring). Also, though RLUIPA is entirely consonant with the Establishment Clause, it may well exceed Congress's authority under either the Spending Clause or the Commerce Clause.

3

The Perspective of the Religious Land Use Applicant

Roman P. Storzer

> There's a lot of animosity. No, that's not a good word. There's a lot of, shall we say, apprehension, says [Mayor] Whitmore, who owns a feed store. "I do not believe this is going to be a terrorist training center. I just haven't heard enough outrage" from Muslims over the Sept. 11 attacks.[1]

Two days after the Ahmadiyya Muslim Community in Walkersville, Maryland, announced plans to build a worship center on an appropriately zoned 224-acre parcel of land, the town introduced an ordinance amendment that would effectively remove places of worship as a permitted use in that zoning district. Community opposition against the Muslim congregation was vociferous and hostile. Comments in letters to the editor, radio show interviews, and blog postings left little doubt that the main reason for the community's opposition was anti-Muslim bias. It was no surprise that the congregation's application was eventually denied.

Among the more printable statements of opposition to the mosque was a suggestion to desecrate the property with pig feces.

> I would think by now some smart local would start a pot-bellied pig business and you could all guess where I would think he or she would dump the waste. Not that someone as peaceful as myself would ever dream of encouraging some-one to (gasp) desecrate a future Islamic holy site, but they are clean pets and walking them down main street is great exercise. If a few Muslim immigrants took offense, I would personally be all broken up inside (NOT).[2]

While Muslims are a popular target of local land use officials,[3] they are not the only minority group to suffer ill treatment. Orthodox Jewish, Hindu, and Buddhist groups are disproportionately represented in reported cases involving zoning of religious land uses.[4] Nontraditional Christian groups are also discriminated against; for example, the Michigan-based Great Lakes Society was denied a special use permit on the basis that its proposed church was not a real "church" under a township's zoning code. A township official in that case was quoted in the media as stating, "It's not a church. The issue is that they're just not a church," even though the Society had been recognized by state and federal authorities—and, ultimately, by an appellate court—as such.[5]

Listening to RLUIPA's opponents, however, an observer unfamiliar with local zoning practices would be left with the impression that such antagonism never existed or, if it once did, no longer exists today.[6] In truth, such hostility is common, and is targeted at many of my clients who are generally unpopular—Orthodox Jewish, Muslim, Hindu, African American Christian, or Buddhist congregations attempting to locate a place of worship in residential, agricultural, or commercial zoning districts.

Differential treatment of minority religious groups in the land use context is one of the key reasons—if not the major one—that Congress unanimously enacted RLUIPA. Over the past eight years, courts, religious organizations, and municipalities have struggled with the implications of this law. Central concepts such as "substantial burden on religious exercise," "compelling governmental interests," and differential treatment between places of worship and similarly situated entities have proven quite difficult to pin down in church zoning cases.[7] However, the emerging trend, at least among the federal courts of appeals, is that evidence of arbitrary and discriminatory decision making on the part of municipal officials often drives the outcome of RLUIPA litigation.

Attorneys—usually land use attorneys familiar with zoning codes and land use law, but not civil rights litigation—are hard pressed to answer a religious institution's seemingly simple question: "Can we worship here?" The only realistic answer continues to be "maybe."

The History, Need, and Constitutionality of RLUIPA

In no other area of government regulation—with perhaps the exception of prisoner rights, which is the other context covered by RLUIPA—is religious exercise impacted as directly as through zoning and planning law. As a colleague once quipped, "Unless you're in a boat or a plane, any religious exercise involves land use."[8] Conflicts are inevitable, and First Amendment lawsuits involving church zoning disputes have been common for many decades, and likely will continue to be for many more.

Moreover, unlike many other civil rights protections such as laws prohibiting sex or race discrimination, there often is not a readily identifiable "bad" actor. Putting discrimination aside, from a municipality's perspective a church use can have several different types of impacts that legitimately can and should be regulated. Churches can impact traffic, historic preservation, economic vitality of a region or neighborhood, and quality of residential life, and these matters have long been accepted as legitimate concerns.[9] Conversely, land use regulation also can have significant effects on churches. From the churches' perspective, zoning ordinances can limit the size of a religious congregation, its ability to grow, what fellowship activities may be permitted, when they are permitted to operate, what types of ministries they can offer, and whether they may educate their children in a religious environment, among many other practical aspects.

Prior to RLUIPA's enactment, the body of law resulting from such conflicts was a muddled series of court decisions that did little to guide church and municipal officials (and their attorneys). Judges ruled, often on very similar facts, that churches enjoyed no First Amendment protection at all, or that churches were immune from zoning regulation, and nearly every point in between.

The tortured history of Free Exercise law in general did little to help. Prior to 1990, "strict scrutiny" judicial review was the norm in analyzing burdens on religious exercise, permitted only when justified by a "compelling governmental interest." In 1990, the Supreme Court handed down the seminal *Employment Division, Department of Human Resources of Oregon v. Smith* decision,[10] which held that the First Amendment does not preclude state enforcement of a neutral and generally applicable criminal prohibition on the use of a controlled substance, where the drug happened to also be used in religious ceremonies. The Court held that the Free Exercise Clause does not "require exemptions from a generally applicable criminal law."[11]

What followed was a struggle between Congress and the Supreme Court that continues to this day. In 1993, Congress passed the Religious Freedom Restoration Act (RFRA),[12] which reestablished strict scrutiny review for Free Exercise claims in all circumstances. In 1997, the high court held that Congress overstepped its bounds in enacting RFRA, at least as it applied to the states.[13] Three years later, and after several failed attempts to pass what was known as the Religious Liberty Protection Act (RLPA), Congress responded with RLUIPA, which is limited to the "land use" and "institutionalized persons" contexts.

RLUIPA was meant to be, among other things, a "visual aid" of existing constitutional protections for churches, municipal officials, and courts, setting out legal rights derived from free exercise, free speech, equal protection, and due process principles. Although prior to the 1980s, courts—especially state courts where these questions were usually litigated—granted great deference to religious organizations, in recent decades they have swung considerably against such claimants. Many courts came to believe that churches enjoyed no religious freedom protection from overly burdensome or unreasonable land use regulation—regardless of how significant the impact was on their practices and beliefs—unless they could demonstrate that such action was motivated by direct religious animus. It can always be demonstrated that a new or expanded place of worship will incrementally increase traffic, increase water usage, cover more square footage, and the like. Therefore, notoriously discretionary zoning processes can lead to denials that can be defended as "rational" and "neutral" on some level. The denial of the Hindu temple or Muslim mosque might ostensibly occur because of "different circumstances," even when Baptist, Methodist, and Catholic churches generating greater impacts were granted more extensive permits. Review in state court was often limited to an "arbitrary and capricious" standard, and court challenges under the First Amendment faced an attitude that "[f]ederal courts are not boards of zoning appeals."[14]

However, RLUIPA has not (yet) succeeded in the goal of eliminating inconsistencies in reported decisions. By far, the most salutary effect of RLUIPA has been to level the playing field between municipalities, religious organizations, and community groups in negotiating successful church zoning outcomes. Although few cases under RLUIPA have actually resulted in courts ordering permits or variances to be granted, many settlements have been reached that accomplish most legitimate goals of all stakeholders. For example, while any increase in traffic, regardless of how slight, could previously have been the basis of an outright permit denial for a church use, the risk of a RLUIPA lawsuit might induce municipal officials to consider alternative methods of satisfying their interests while still permitting the religious exercise to exist in some form. There is also an incentive for the religious organization and the community to resolve their differences amicably.

Furthermore, it has been my experience that while councilpersons, planning commissioners, and members of zoning boards—who are elected themselves or appointed by elected officials—may privately have little problem with a proposed religious land use, they are accountable to a constituency that may be unreasonably opposed to such a plan. Opposition may stem from religious bigotry or from typical NIMBYism, that familiar acronym for "Not in My Backyard." Certain additional concessions made by the applicant, combined with pressure from a federal judge, often provide decision makers with the political cover of being "forced" to accept a compromise.[15]

After eight years of RLUIPA, there can be little doubt that lawsuits are disproportionately brought by minority or nontraditional faith groups, often after great soul searching by their clergy and boards. While the local First Presbyterian Church will typically include many members of the community and might even be represented on the city council or zoning board by its members, a Hindu or Muslim congregation—likely comprised of immigrants and racial minorities—will often have less political acumen. In the context of a RLUIPA decision, Judge Posner of the Seventh Circuit recognized "the vulnerability of religious institutions—especially those that are not affiliated with the mainstream Protestant sects or the Roman Catholic Church—to subtle forms of discrimination when, as in the case of the grant or denial of zoning variances, a state delegates essentially standardless discretion to nonprofessionals operating without procedural safeguards."[16]

Also placing the religious land use applicant at a disadvantage is the possibility that the great majority of those engaged in the democratic local land use process might feel that there is no advantage to be gained by the proposed place of worship, unlike the construction of a Wal-Mart, gas station, or recreation center. Why should they be required to accept even a 5 percent increase in traffic Sunday mornings if they receive no benefit from such a use? Or, as one opponent to the Muslim community in Walkersville wrote to the local newspaper (in between diatribes against Muslims): "When the town of Walkersville has its carnival, we have traffic issues, but there is a difference: The town does benefit from this."[17] While the provision of attorneys' fees is a lightning rod for opponents' criticisms,[18] the possibility of a substantial award often leads to just and equitable results where the municipality otherwise sees no downside to placating a hostile citizenry by excluding an unpopular (or simply unfamiliar and politically irrelevant) place of worship.

Some academics—and, of course, many municipal officials—believe that RLUIPA's land use provisions are unconstitutional. However, every court that has ruled upon this issue—at least, those courts that have not been reversed—has disagreed, including several federal courts of appeals. The reasoning of such decisions is relatively straightforward: the statute only applies where Congress possesses the authority to regulate, that is, by using its Spending or

Commerce Clause powers, or where it has the power to enforce the provisions of the Fourteenth Amendment. The sole remaining rational basis[19] for a challenge to RLUIPA—that it violates the Establishment Clause of the First Amendment by favoring religion and religious actors over nonreligion—has been answered satisfactorily (at least for all but the most diehard opponents) by the Supreme Court in *Cutter v. Wilkinson*.[20] There, the Court held that Congress can accommodate religious exercise in the prisons (but is not required to accommodate similar nonreligious practices), without "establishing" religion. The principle is equally applicable in the land use context.

Although the Supreme Court has not yet formally upheld the land use provisions of RLUIPA, it will likely do so if and when such a case comes before it. Opposing a church land use based on an assumption that RLUIPA will be held unconstitutional would be ill advised.

Practical Application of the RLUIPA Statute

Although the enactment of RLUIPA has reinvigorated church zoning litigation, the same difficulties have arisen in adjudicating such claims. The predominant issue in most RLUIPA cases is the existence, or lack thereof, of a substantial burden on religious exercise. The statute requires a claimant to make a prima facie case that a government has "impose[d] or implement[ed] a land use regulation in a manner that imposes a substantial burden on the religious exercise of a person, including a religious assembly or institution."[21] Generally, the scenario involves denial of a land use permit or variance to build or expand a place of worship, or a related structure such as a religious school or fellowship hall. Courts are faced with what might appear to be a Hobson's choice of adopting a principle where the denial of the use of any particular parcel of land as a place of worship may create a substantial burden on religious exercise or, alternatively, that no substantial burden exists unless the applicant can demonstrate that it is unable to worship elsewhere.

The potential problem with the first approach is the belief that any land use denial may therefore result in a RLUIPA violation—the "immunity from zoning laws" threat often raised by RLUIPA opponents.[22] There are several responses to this objection. First, municipalities are always free to regulate in a manner that protects compelling governmental interests, so long as they use the means that are least restrictive on religious exercise to achieve such interests.[23] Churches that claim exemptions from certain fire or building safety regulations or projects that may cause legitimate traffic safety problems may be denied. Second, burdens that are not "substantial" do not violate RLUIPA. Requests such as height limitation or setback waivers are not protected by RLUIPA if the religious exercise of the applicant is not affected, provided the refusal is not discriminatory or arbitrary. Third, if there is a genuine conflict between a congregation's ability to worship and the less than compelling interests of a community, such as aesthetic interests, lowering property values, or generating commercial activity, it is the clear intent of Congress that religious liberty is the superior interest that must be protected. However, it is usually the case that the legitimate and reasonable interests of a community can be met by some means other than outright denial of a zoning permit.

The other approach—that no substantial burden on religious exercise exists unless the applicant can prove that there is no alternative property within the jurisdiction on which it can locate—is more troubling. One example is the Ninth Circuit's suggestion that a landowner's religious exercise was not substantially burdened by a denial of rezoning because "there is no evidence in the record demonstrating that College was precluded from using other sites within the city."[24] Having been adopted by some courts, this narrow interpretation effectively nullifies RLUIPA's protections of religious liberty and renders a federal statute meaningless. It would certainly be difficult, if not impossible, to demonstrate that no other property is available within a jurisdiction. Even if an applicant did so, a court may opine that any land would become available at a high enough price. "Whatever specific difficulties plaintiff church claims to have encountered, they are the same ones that face all land users. The harsh reality of the marketplace sometimes dictates that certain facilities are not available to those who desire them."[25]

The distinction, of course, is that the activities of other "land users" are not protected by the Constitution and by a specific Act of Congress. In no other area of free exercise law does such an unattainable standard exist. A government employee forced to work on her Sabbath does not lose her Free Exercise claim on the basis that she may seek employment elsewhere. Nor does a student forced to participate in sex education despite religious objection lose his argument because he is free to attend a different school. Yet, courts continue to occasionally require this evidence from the religious land use applicant. Finally, this approach would render the "Substantial Burdens" provision wholly redundant because of RLUIPA's "Exclusion and Limits" section, which requires that "[n] o government shall impose or implement a land use regulation that—(A) totally excludes religious assemblies from a jurisdiction," violating generally accepted rules of statutory construction.[26]

Although such inconsistencies continue to abound in this area of law, a pattern has emerged from the dozens of cases that have made their way to the court system. This is the general rule that in an area of law with few—if any—established practical rules, courts are aware of the equities in cases brought before them and tend to steer the results accordingly. When a church attempts in good faith to resolve legitimate municipal interests in its effort to build a place of worship, its claims are generally favored, especially when such attempts are unreasonably rebuffed by the municipality. However, when an attempt is made to bypass the permitting requirements of a zoning code, courts tend to develop principles supporting a negative outcome for the applicant.

Decisions rendered by the Second, Seventh, and Ninth Circuit Courts of Appeals plainly demonstrate this principle. Each of these courts has been presented with one case where the RLUIPA claimant had been found not to have made an exhaustive effort to comply with zoning requirements, and a later case where another (or, in one circumstance, the same) applicant had done so. In each Circuit, the first case did not result in a determination of a RLUIPA violation, but the second case did.

The first example involved the Seventh Circuit's rejection of a challenge brought by various religious organizations to the city of Chicago's zoning ordinance, which required churches to apply for special use permits to locate in certain zoning districts.[27] The court—which specifically noted that "each of the five individual plaintiff churches has successfully located within Chicago's city limits"—held that "expend[ing] considerable time and money . . . does not entitle them to relief under RLUIPA's substantial burden provision."[28] The opposite result was reached in the Seventh Circuit's next RLUIPA decision, *Saints Constantine and Helen Greek Orthodox Church v. City of New Berlin*,[29] where it held that denial of a rezoning application did violate RLUIPA. The court distinguished *C.L.U.B.* as a case involving a challenge to the *requirement* of obtaining a zoning permit.

> The Church in our case doesn't argue that having to apply for what amounts to a zoning variance to be allowed to build in a residential area is a substantial burden. It complains instead about having either to sell the land that it bought in New Berlin and find a suitable alternative parcel or be subjected to unreasonable delay by having to restart the permit process to satisfy the Planning Commission about a contingency for which the Church has already provided complete satisfaction.[30]

The strong evidence, if not outright discrimination, of arbitrary and capricious behavior on the part of municipal officials was a considerable factor in the decision of *Saints Constantine and Helen*. The court noted "the whiff of bad faith arising from the Planning Commission's rejection of a solution that would have eliminated the City's only legitimate concern," "the City['s] flaunting as it were its own incompetence," "the mayor['s] playing a delaying game," and its belief that "repeated legal errors by the City's officials casts doubt on their good faith."[31] There is little doubt that such circumstances, although perhaps not directly related to the question of whether a substantial burden on the Church's religious exercise was caused by the rezoning denial, influenced the court's decision.

Similar to *C.L.U.B.*, a decision by the Ninth Circuit Court of Appeals rejected plaintiff San Jose Christian College's claim that the denial of its rezoning application to construct a religious education facility violated RLUIPA.[32] The city of Morgan Hill argued that it rejected the college's application because it failed to comply with the city's requirements for a rezoning application, while the college argued that such denial precluded it from using the property for religious education. The court of appeals sided with the city, reasoning (under the Seventh Circuit's *C.L.U.B.* decision) that:

> [I]t appears that College is simply adverse to complying with the PUD ordinance's requirements. The City's ordinance imposes no restriction whatsoever on College's religious exercise; it merely requires College to submit a complete application, as is required of all applicants. Should College comply with this request, it is not at all apparent that its rezoning application will be denied.[33]

Two years later, the same court was presented with a scenario in which the plaintiff had submitted not only one completed application, but two, and was rejected both times.

> The net effect of the County's two denials—including their underlying rationales and disregard for Guru Nanak's accepted mitigation conditions—is to shrink the large amount of land theoretically available to Guru Nanak under the Zoning Code to several scattered parcels that the County may or may not ultimately approve. Because the County's actions have to a significantly great extent lessened the prospect of Guru Nanak being able to construct a temple in the future, the County has imposed a substantial burden on Guru Nanak's religious exercise.[34]

Two aspects of the *Guru Nanak Sikh Society* decision are notable. First, as in *Saints Constantine and Helen*, the court was aware of the "inconsistent decision-making" of the county, which rejected the society's first application to locate in a residential district because of complaints by residents of increased noise and traffic, and rejected its second application in a sparsely populated agricultural district because it would contribute to "leapfrog development."[35] A reader of the opinion is left with the clear impression that the equities weighed heavily in the society's favor against a county that appeared to not want the temple located anywhere within its jurisdiction. Second, the society made every effort to mitigate any potential impacts on legitimate county interests.

> Similarly, during both of its CUP application processes, Guru Nanak agreed to every mitigation condition the Planning Division found necessary to recommend the

> land entitlements. Nevertheless, in denying the second application, the Board of Supervisors neither related why any of such mitigation conditions were inadequate nor suggested additional conditions that would render satisfactory Guru Nanak's application.[36]

These factors were not present in the *San Jose Christian College* litigation. Critical, again, to the society's success in its RLUIPA claim was the suggestion of discrimination and bad faith by the county.

Finally, the Second Circuit heard two appeals, and issued two different opinions in the same litigation involving the Westchester Day School of Mamaroneck, New York.[37] This case involved the expansion of an existing Jewish day school rather than the construction of a new place of worship or religious school. Following the district court's grant of summary judgment for the school, the Second Circuit originally reversed, holding that the school had not established that it received a "complete denial"—in other words, it believed that there existed "the possibility of approving a modified application designed to cure the problems and deficiencies cited by the Board."[38] The case was remanded for trial. After a bench trial before Judge Connor of the Southern District of New York and judgment in the school's favor, the court of appeals affirmed the decision.

As with the Ninth and Seventh Circuits, the court did not focus on the actual burden on the school's religious exercise, but on what it described as the village's "arbitrary blindness to the facts."[39]

> The same reasoning that precludes a religious organization from demonstrating substantial burden in the neutral application of legitimate land use restrictions may, in fact, support a substantial burden claim where land use restrictions are imposed on the religious institution arbitrarily, capriciously, or unlawfully. The arbitrary application of laws to religious organizations may reflect bias or discrimination against religion.[40]

Relevant to the finding of substantial burden was various evidence demonstrating bad faith, including "a willful attempt to mislead the zoning board," "allegations of deficiencies in the school's traffic study [that] were also unsupported by the evidence before it," "concern about lack of adequate parking [that] was based on the zoning board's own miscalculation," and "speculation about future expansion, without a basis in fact."[41] The suggestion of bad faith again carried the day.

Discrimination and arbitrariness should be relevant in RLUIPA and free exercise litigation; however, there are specific provisions other than the "substantial burdens" provision designed to remedy such wrongdoing.[42] It is difficult to understand why a denial of a land use permit creates a more significant burden on a church's religious exercise because it was motivated by bias. A denial of a special use permit based on serious traffic concerns creates the same burden on religious exercise (although certainly one that is more justifiable) as one motivated by religious bigotry. The fact that "discrimination" issues have become relevant for substantial burden claims—even though the statute does not explicitly make discrimination an element of the violation—underscores the difficulty faced by courts charged with establishing a principled standard for determining whether substantial burdens exist, while avoiding legitimate *reductio ad absurdum* arguments of "immunity from zoning regulations" on the one hand, and rendering a duly enacted federal statute meaningless on the other.

Regardless, potential church litigants would be well advised to observe permitting requirements and, especially where zoning permits are a discretionary process, to attempt to resolve the stated concerns of neighbors, municipal officials, and other stakeholders. Where such efforts have been made, continued rejections increase the likelihood that discrimination or arbitrary and capricious behavior is the cause. Evidence of that becomes the most powerful tool in convincing a court of the existence of a "substantial burden."

A second difficulty often raised in RLUIPA proceedings is the question of what constitutes a "compelling governmental interest," which can justify a substantial burden on religious exercise.[43] Again, reported decisions have been inconsistent. Traditionally, "no showing merely of a rational relationship to some colorable state interest would suffice; in this highly sensitive constitutional area, only the gravest abuses, endangering paramount interest, give occasion for permissible limitation."[44] The interest required is the same as the interest necessary to justify racially discriminatory laws.

Some courts, however, continue to follow a sporadic pre-RLUIPA line of cases that held as a general matter that "a municipal body clearly has a compelling interest in enacting and enforcing fair and reasonable zoning regulations."[45] These courts ignore the specific municipal interests at stake and, equally importantly, how the proposed religious use would actually impact those interests. Any aspect of a municipality's zoning code—whether relating to safety or aesthetics—becomes, per se, "compelling."

This approach is clearly wrong. As the Second Circuit held in *Westchester Day School v. Village of Mamaroneck,* municipalities "must show a compelling interest in imposing the burden on religious exercise in the particular case at hand, not a compelling interest in general."[46] The Supreme Court also held, in a case involving RFRA, that it "look[s] beyond broadly formulated interests justifying the general applicability of government mandates and scrutinize[s] the asserted harm of granting specific exemptions to particular religious claimants."[47] Once a substantial burden on religious exercise has been determined to exist, the burden shifts to the municipality to prove the existence of an actual—not generalized—interest of paramount importance that requires denial of a land use permit.[48] Such analysis often requires both sides to present evidence from consultants and professional staff, expert testimony, and review of treatment of similarly situated entities.

The Road Ahead

Unfortunately, both sides can expect inconsistent application of RLUIPA's substantive concepts to continue. Litigants may take comfort in the knowledge that federal judges reward good behavior—on both sides—in the church zoning process, and therefore the commandment to "love thy neighbor" takes on special significance for churches and municipalities engaged in such efforts. Nevertheless, barring unexpected clarification by the Supreme Court—which certainly has not been forthcoming in the last several decades—RLUIPA litigation promises to remain a chaotic, time-consuming, and expensive affair.

Notes

1. Andrea Stone, *Muslim Sect Resisted in Md.*, USA TODAY, Sept. 30, 2007 (updated Oct. 1, 2007), *available at* http://www.usatoday.com/news/religion/2007-09-30-muslims_N.htm at p.3A.
2. Muslim Sect Causes Stir in Walkersville, http://doctorbulldog.wordpress.com/2007/08/31/muslim-sect-causes-stir-in-walkersville/ (Aug. 31, 2007, 7:07 EST).
3. *Albanian Associated Fund v. Twp. of Wayne*, 2007 WL 2904194, at *7 (D.N.J. Oct. 1, 2007) ("The circumstances of this case and the manner in which the plaintiffs' property was pursued, at the very least, supports an indication of discriminatory or improper purpose for which plaintiffs are entitled to inquire into the Council's motives in condemning the plaintiffs' property. . . .").
4. The testimony of one village official in Suffern, New York, is remarkable only for its honesty: "Q. Are you aware of the general public concern with the Hasidic Jewish population moving into the Town of Ramapo and the Villages? A. From some people, yes. Q. Do you share that concern? . . . A. Yes." *Bikur Cholim v. Vill. of Suffern*, Civ. No. 05-10759 (S.D.N.Y., complaint filed Jan 3, 2006) (deposition transcript on file with author).
5. Barton Deiters, *Church Sues, Claims Bias in Building Ban*, GRAND RAPIDS PRESS, Apr. 2, 2003, at C4. Although the Great Lakes Society was finally vindicated in court, it came at the price of most of its congregation, five years (and counting) of litigation, hundreds of thousands of dollars in attorneys' fees, and the health of its pastor.
6. Marci Hamilton, *The Federal Government's Intervention on Behalf of Religious Entities in Local Land Use Disputes: Why It's a Terrible Idea*, FINDLAW, Nov. 6, 2003, *available at* http://writ.news.findlaw.com/hamilton/20031106.html. ("What about subsequent RLUIPA court cases? Might they not reveal discrimination, even if the legislative history does not? Well, they might—but in fact, they don't.").
7. The term "church" is used broadly herein to describe any place of worship, including Jewish synagogues, Hindu and Sikh Temples, Buddhist meditation facilities, and Muslim mosques.
8. Anthony R. Picarello, Jr., former president of the Becket Fund for Religious Liberty, and currently general counsel for the U.S. Conference of Catholic Bishops.

9. *See Vill. of Euclid, Ohio v. Ambler Realty Co.*, 272 U.S. 365 (1926); *Vill. of Belle Terre v. Boraas*, 416 U.S. 1, 9 (1974).
10. 494 U.S. 872 (1990).
11. *Id.* at 884. The holding was subsequently applied to civil as well as criminal laws. Whether zoning laws and their application are "neutral" and "generally applicable"—and thus subject to *Smith*'s rule—is a question that courts continue to struggle with, and is often implicated in RLUIPA lawsuits. 42 U.S.C.A. § 2000cc(a)(2)(C).
12. 42 U.S.C.A. § 2000bb et seq.
13. *City of Boerne v. Flores*, 521 U.S. 507 (1997). RFRA continues to apply to federal action that burdens religious exercise.
14. *Civil Liberties for Urban Believers v. City of Chicago,* 342 F.3d 752, 767 (7th Cir. 2003) [hereinafter *C.L.U.B.*].
15. As one appellate panel suggested, "We are sure that with the district judge's help the parties can work out a deal that will lift a substantial burden from the Church's shoulders without impairing any legitimate interest of the City." *Saints Constantine & Helen Greek Orthodox Church v. City of New Berlin*, 396 F.3d 895, 901 (7th Cir. 2005).
16. *Id.* at 900.
17. Terry Spicer, Letter to the Editor, FREDERICK NEWS-POST, Oct. 29, 2007, at A8.
18. *See* Marci Hamilton, *Religion's Financial Windfalls in the Bush and Clinton Eras*, FINDLAW, June 12, 2006, *available at* http://writ.news.findlaw.com/hamilton/20060612.html (last visited Mar. 21, 2009).
19. Various other arguments, such as those made under the Tenth Amendment, have been made against RLUIPA and summarily rejected by the courts.
20. 544 U.S. 709 (2005).
21. 42 U.S.C.A. § 2000cc(a)(1).
22. *But see Corp. of the Presiding Bishop of the Church of Jesus Christ of Latter-Day Saints v. City of West Linn*, 86 P.3d 1140, 1149 (Or. App. 2004) ("[T]he only sense in which RLUIPA properly can be characterized as conferring 'immunity' from land use

regulations is in the sense of partial protection from those constraints.").

23. 42 U.S.C.A. § 2000cc(a)(1)(A).
24. *San Jose Christian Coll. v. City of Morgan Hill*, 360 F.3d 1024 (9th Cir. 2004).
25. *C.L.U.B.*, 342 F.3d at 761 (quoting *Love Church v. City of Evanston*, 896 F.2d 1082, 1086 (7th Cir. 1990)).
26. 42 U.S.C.A. § 2000cc(b)(3).
27. *C.L.U.B.*, 342 F.3d 752.
28. *Id.* at 761–62.
29. 396 F.3d 895 (7th Cir. 2005).
30. *Id.* at 900.
31. *Id.* at 899–901.
32. *San Jose Christian Coll.*, 360, F.3d 1024.
33. *Id.* at 1035.
34. *Guru Nanak Sikh Soc'y of Yuma City v. County of Sutter*, 456 F.3d 978, 991–92 (9th Cir. 2006) (footnote omitted).
35. *Id.* at 989–92.
36. *Id.* at 991.
37. *Westchester Day School v. Village of Mamaroneck*, 386 F.3d 183 (2d Cir. 2004) [hereinafter *WDS I*]; *Westchester Day School v. Village of Mamaroneck*, 504 F.3d 338 (2d Cir. 2007) [hereinafter *WDS II*].
38. *WDS I*, 386 F.3d at 187.
39. *WDS II*, 504 F.3d at 352.
40. *Id.* at 350.
41. *Id.* at 351.
42. 42 U.S.C.A. § 2000cc(b)(2) ("(2) Nondiscrimination—No government shall impose or implement a land use regulation that discriminates against any assembly or institution on the basis of religion or religious denomination."); 42 U.S.C.A. § 2000cc(b)(3)(B) ("(3) Exclusions and limits—No government shall impose or implement a land use regulation that— . . . (B) unreasonably limits religious assemblies, institutions, or structures within a jurisdiction.").
43. 42 U.S.C.A. § 2000cc(a)(1).
44. *Sherbert v. Verner*, 374 U.S. 398, 403 (1963) (internal citation omitted).

45. *Greater Bible Way Temple of Jackson v. City of Jackson*, 478 Mich. 373, 403, 733 N.W.2d 734 (2007) (internal citation omitted).
46. *WDS II*, 504 F.3d at 353.
47. *Gonzales v. O Centro Espirita Beneficente Uniao Do Vegetal*, 546 U.S. 418, 431 (2006).
48. 42 U.S.C.A. § 2000cc-2(b).

4

The Unintended Consequences RLUIPA Has Visited on Residential Neighborhoods

Marci A. Hamilton

The most dangerous aspect of legislation is often its unintended consequences. The Religious Land Use and Institutionalized Persons Act (RLUIPA) magnifies this peril because its constitutional doctrinal language does not lend itself to the searching inquiry that the public interest would otherwise demand. RLUIPA states that local and state governments must not "substantially burden" religious entities through "land use law," and that there should be "equal treatment" and "nondiscrimination." These vague pronouncements—which are actually parroted constitutional law terminology—do not invite the debate that members of Congress should have had when they passed it.[1] Nor do they alert homeowners to the potential threat posed by the law.

Imagine what the press and public reaction would have been if the bill had been entitled "A Bill to Permit

Religious Landowners to Do Whatever They Want in Residential Neighborhoods and to Subsidize Lawyers for Religious Landowners with an Attorney's Fee Provision," instead of RLUIPA. That would have been a title no less misleading, and a law that the members of Congress might well have examined with care, unlike their treatment of RLUIPA.

With the talismanic and comforting constitutional language dulling their policy antennae, members of Congress did not raise the questions they should have—while homeowners remained blissfully unaware that a federal religious liberty bill was about to play havoc with the land use rules in place in their neighborhoods. The result has been misery for many homeowners and neighborhoods.

The Legislative History Behind RLUIPA Related to Residential Use[2]

The value of a residential neighborhood was recognized by the Supreme Court in 1974 when it explained:

> The regimes of boarding houses, fraternity houses, and the like present urban problems. More people occupy a given space; more cars rather continuously pass by; more cars are parked; noise travels with crowds.
>
> A quiet place where yards are wide, people few, and motor vehicles restricted are legitimate guidelines in a land use project addressed to family needs. This goal is a permissible one within *Berman v. Parker*. The police power is not confined to elimination of filth, stench, and unhealthy places. It is ample to lay out zones where family values, youth values, and the blessings of quiet seclusion and clean air make the area a sanctuary for people.[3]

During the enactment of RLUIPA, questions should have been raised regarding how the bill would impact homeowners. The inevitable conflict between RLUIPA's expansion of the rights of religious landowners and the rights of residential neighbors under existing land use law did not trigger examination by Congress. Yet, it is no secret in this country that many neighborhoods have existing churches, synagogues, mosques, or other houses of worship. (For ease of reference, the term "church" will be used throughout to indicate all houses of worship, regardless of denomination or belief.) Nor should it be a surprise to learn that churches, which were once limited-use buildings, have dramatically expanded outreach and use. Whereas there was a time when a church was largely a quiet, park-like neighbor, most churches today offer programming to members and nonmembers, sometimes on a daily basis. Religious entities often use their buildings at later hours than was formerly common, with midnight basketball being just one example. Homeowners and land use planners, therefore, were already struggling with the question of how to fit a busy religious use into a residential neighborhood when Congress inserted RLUIPA into the mix.

Land use law exists, in part, to make conflicting uses compatible. A typical means to this end is to impose reasonable and neutral rules that regulate the effect of the more intense use on the less intense use. Standard and legitimate concerns in residential neighborhoods include traffic, fire safety, density, light, and noise. Some neighborhoods have legitimate concerns about views—whether of the ocean or the mountains, the residential "character" of the neighborhood, and the preservation of open space. While religious entities have had to concede that the first set of concerns might be legitimate in some circumstances (although they typically fight any justification for land use law that burdens religious development), they have persistently characterized the latter set of concerns as nothing more than "aesthetics," which should never weigh more heavily than the religious entity's demands for increased use. Similarly, the notion that property value should weigh in the land use calculus is treated as inappropriate.

The record behind RLUIPA is replete with statements by and for religious entities unhappy with the normal land use process, but it conspicuously lacks critical inquiry into RLUIPA's effects on residential neighborhoods. There are few references to residential neighborhoods, but virtually all take the religious body's perspective. None come from members of Congress, which means that at no time did a member of Congress consider his or her constituents' interest in their homes.[4] Indeed, there were no hearings directed at RLUIPA alone; rather, all legislative history is taken from hearings regarding its predecessor, the Religious Liberty Protection Act

(RLPA), which never became law. The members were prompted to take these considerations into account by my testimony, where I stated:

> RLPA is a blank check for religion. It took the ACLU approximately five years to fathom that RFRA (and now RLPA) is a threat to the civil rights laws. What other hidden agendas lie in this across-the-board preference for religion? For example, there are religions that hope to run day care centers without having to satisfy the onerous health and safety regulations under which secular day care centers operate. RLPA would have made that easier. Others hope to operate soup kitchens or hold worship services in residential neighborhoods without having to abide by certain zoning and land use regulations.[5]

RLPA, with its enormous breadth, did not go forward as drafted. RLPA would have applied to most laws, and it was defeated largely by children's advocacy and municipal organizations. Lobbyists on the land use and prison issues, however, did not desist after losing the legal battle to defend the RFRA in court and RLPA in Congress. Their success was assured when RLUIPA, the veritable sausage of religious liberty legislation, passed. Congress did not hold new hearings once RLPA had been transformed into RLUIPA.

A statement by Professor Cole Durham, Jr., of Brigham Young University, summarized the prevailing attitude during the hearings related to land use. The strong implication is that most land use denials are motivated by discriminatory intent, rather than standard land use principles; he also prioritized reasons for denial with traffic, fire, noise, and disturbance having some potential value, but property values and density constituting "crasser grounds" for denial.

> Human experience teaches us that public officials, when faced with pressure to bar church uses by those residing in a residential neighborhood, tend to avoid any appearance of an anti-religious stance and temper their decision by carefully couching their grounds for refusal to permit such use in terms of traffic dangers, fire hazards and noise

> and disturbance, rather than on such crasser grounds as lessening of property values or loss of open space or entry of strangers into the neighborhood or undue crowding of the area. Under such circumstances it is necessary to carefully scrutinize the reasons advanced for a denial to insure that they are real and not merely pretexts used to preclude the exercise of constitutionally protected privileges.[6]

In fact, RLUIPA has hit residential neighborhoods time after time, and many neighbors of ambitious religious land use projects are bitter that Congress has undermined the residential character of their neighborhoods.

RLUIPA should have state and local governments up in arms, because one of the last strongholds of local control lies in land use.[7] There is nothing more local than land, and when it is land on which a home is situated, states' rights and federalism should cry out for restrictions on congressional power. Landowners should not have to lobby Washington, but rather should be regulated within and by their respective communities.

Private home ownership is part and parcel of the American Dream. Not long ago, members of Congress railed against the Supreme Court's decision in *Kelo v. City of New London*,[8] because they believed it undermined the rights of homeowners against eminent domain. "The Supreme Court voted last week to undo private property rights and to empower governments to kick people out of their homes and give them to someone else because they feel like it," said House Majority Leader Tom DeLay, Texas Republican. "No court that denies property rights will long respect and recognize other basic human rights."[9] Ironically, Congress has done the same to residential homeowners by enacting RLUIPA and allowing it to apply in residential neighborhoods. RLUIPA has had an unintended and unfortunate impact on homeowners.

Does RLUIPA Preempt Local Land Use Law?

One interpretation of RLUIPA is that it is intended to "preempt" local land use law, as though it provides religious landowners and project developers the ability to trump local law as of right. Early responses from local governments, which were cowed by the legislation, reflect this attitude. The most extreme case was one in Hancock Park, California, which is a neighborhood in Los Angeles where Congregation Etz Chaim sought to have a synagogue. Under the Los Angeles code, a house of worship was not permitted in the residential neighborhood without a conditional use permit. All those who ruled on the issue, from the initial local proceedings to the end of the state litigation, held that it was an inappropriate use.[10]

Having filed in federal court as well, the congregation amended its complaint after RLUIPA took effect. The city then made a 180-degree turn in response to the congregation's invocation of RLUIPA. It entered into a settlement agreement in secret proceedings and, through that settlement agreement, purported to grant approval to the congregation. Residents, thinking that the state proceedings had settled the issue and receiving no notice from the city that a reversal of the prior decision was under consideration, were shocked to learn that the congregation was, after all, going to be able to operate a synagogue in a residential neighborhood.

In the vast majority of cases, neighborhoods are unable to support the cost of litigation in federal court. Therefore, if the local government is not in agreement with the neighbors, they are usually sidelined, as in a case from Castle Hills, Texas. The situation in Los Angeles was different, though, and the neighborhood formed an organization to fight the city's about face, calling itself the League of Residential Neighborhood Advocates (LRNA).[11]

The residents filed a lawsuit challenging the proposed use on grounds that public notice was never provided for the new permit, and challenging the notion that the city could unilaterally overturn a land use determination that had been fully litigated through the state courts. The district court ruled in the city's (and the congregation's) favor, finding that it had the authority to approve the religious use in order to avoid RLUIPA litigation.[12]

The import of the federal district court's decision was to show the neighbors that they could no longer trust that the application of standard, long-settled land use law would result in the denial of a religious land use, even where the denial was repeatedly affirmed in the state courts. The mere invocation of RLUIPA by an entity could transform a denial into an approval. Moreover, the turnaround could occur without the usual notice, public hearings, and input from neighbors that would otherwise be required when an incompatible use was sought within a residential zone. To the neighbors it seemed as though they had walked through Alice's Looking Glass into a world devoid of the legal principles they previously could count on to protect them.

After seven years, the neighborhood finally prevailed when the Ninth Circuit ruled that the city could not simply and unilaterally abandon its land use code, just because it faced a claim under RLUIPA.[13] The effect of the decision is that mere invocation of RLUIPA by a plaintiff cannot justify a settlement that preempted valid state and local laws. Rather "a district court must find that there has been or will be an *actual* violation of that federal law" before a municipality may take the position that it is entitled to disregard the allegedly conflicting state law.[14]

The LRNA case is unusual in two respects. First, a neighborhood was able to vindicate its rights in federal court because there were enough neighbors fighting for the cause and because they could afford it. Second, because those neighbors took up that fight, we now know about this particular example of a local government treating a permit applicant's mere invocation of RLUIPA as if it completely preempted local laws and procedures. It is impossible to know how many times local governments have made concessions to RLUIPA to the detriment of neighbors who lack the sophistication or financial means to oppose it. In those circumstances, once the local government and the church have reached a deal, there may be no one in a position—financially or even legally—to challenge the government's acquiescence to RLUIPA.

Anecdotally, I have heard a number of these stories, but most occurred relatively soon after RLUIPA became law. Some cities refused to succumb, and fought RLUIPA lawsuits. Once case law began to appear on various aspects of the statute, it became harder for city attorneys to advise total capitulation. Cities won in significant cases, especially with regard to whether the religious entity had proved "substantial burden."

Federal Oversight Increases Over Local Land Use Disputes

RLUIPA dramatically increased federal intervention and oversight in local land use decision making. Before RLUIPA was enacted, federal courts infrequently encountered standard land use law issues because such issues were typically considered the provenance of local bodies and state courts. The one arena in which the federal courts were dealing directly with local land use was through the federal Fair Housing Act, which prohibits discrimination only on the basis of race, color, religion, and national origin, and has been in place since 1968. Prior to RLUIPA, although there were no cases at the United States Supreme Court, and very few in the lower courts, federal courts were familiar with the possibility that the Free Exercise Clause might be applied to prohibit intentional discrimination in the land use context.

RLUIPA, in contrast, forced federal courts to look at the nuts and bolts of land use and then to pass judgment.[15] Rather than assessing claims of intentional discrimination, the courts found themselves being asked to determine whether a church should be permitted to add a fourth story in a residential neighborhood or whether a private individual could hold large weekly gatherings in his home for prayer and worship. Issues like traffic impact, intensity of use, setbacks, and lot and building size come to the fore in such cases, and federal judges are neither trained for nor particularly prepared to make such judgment calls. Until RLUIPA, these were the cases state judges invariably decided. In most jurisdictions, the states have developed doctrines to ensure that land use authorities do not act arbitrarily or capriciously, and that neutral principles are applied when denials are rendered.

Although I cannot prove the causal link, I believe that this relative unfamiliarity with the underlying law (and the extraordinary attention to detail demanded by land use and zoning law) accounts for the slow movement of RLUIPA cases through the federal courts. By contrast, before many federal appellate courts had even heard their first RLUIPA case, a constitutional challenge to the prison provisions of the statute had been addressed by the Supreme Court in *Cutter v. Wilkinson*, which reserved the issue of whether RLUIPA is constitutional in the land use context.[16] The evidence is that the federal courts have been out of their element in hearing and deciding most of the RLUIPA cases.

One particularly egregious example of inappropriately zealous federal involvement concerns a dispute over the repeated expansion of a Baptist church in a residential neighborhood in Castle Hills, Texas. The primary issue was a proposal to expand the use of a fourth floor and to create additional parking in a neighborhood with significant rainwater runoff issues. Following the city's denial of approval for the church's land use application, the church filed suit in federal court, making RLUIPA and related constitutional and statutory claims. The district court handed a win to each side. With respect to the changed use of the building's fourth floor, it found a substantial burden, and granted the church's section 1983, RLUIPA, and First Amendment claims; however, the court found that the church failed to demonstrate a substantial burden as to the city's denial of the additional parking.[17] Neighbors were unhappy, and braced for an appeal of the parking lot issue; but no appeal was filed. In most federal cases, when a party abandons its appeal from a trial court decision, the judge concludes that he no longer has jurisdiction over the dispute, and dismisses the case. The federal district court judge in this case, however, saw an opportunity to ensure that the parties would not have future disputes, and has retained jurisdiction over the case, for more than three years thus far at the time of this writing. The judge formed an ad hoc committee composed of interested parties, and the neighbors were largely shut out of the "conciliation" process. The neighbors have been fortunate to have a local attorney attend a few of the hearings on their behalf, but they have not been able to participate fully in the process because, like residents of most other neighborhoods in America, they do not have the money to vigorously pursue federal litigation.

The federal district court judge in the *Castle Hills* case has assumed the community's role in settling and resolving land use tensions. Despite the fully developed land use procedures available in Castle Hills, he found it appropriate to continue looking over everyone's shoulder after his appointed role should have ended. This is an extreme, but telling, example of RLUIPA's intrusion into local affairs.

The Imbalance of Power Between Residential Homeowners and Religious Entities

Neighbors are at a disadvantage when they object to a land use project involving a religious entity because they typically cannot afford federal litigation. There was a time when a church could not afford litigation either, and would have negotiated or found a more suitable location, rather than fight in court. But the attorneys' fee provisions in RLUIPA have altered this equation. Now churches can pursue litigation with the promise of having their attorneys' fees paid by the local government defendant if the church wins. This places the neighbors in an even worse position.

RLUIPA provides that "the court, in its discretion, may allow the prevailing party . . . a reasonable attorney's fee as part of the costs. . . ."[18] In other words, local governments have to pay the churches' attorneys if the latter prevail. In actual practice, they also have been forced to pay attorneys' fees in order to obtain a settlement as well. Therefore, the only time the city is not forced to pay both sides' attorneys in a RLUIPA suit is when it has a clear-cut final win in the federal court. That is hard to accomplish, because many times the religious organization merely has to threaten an appeal in federal court, with all its attendant costs, and the local government will agree to a settlement. Groups such as the Becket Fund and certain law firms have pursued RLUIPA clients, and, in many circumstances, bankrolled the litigation. The result has been that churches are now more inclined to challenge land use determinations than they were prior to RLUIPA's enactment, because it can be virtually cost free.

The prospect of having to pay a plaintiff's attorneys' fees is a strong deterrent to a local government's enforcement of land use codes. Incumbent in every denial of a church's land use application is the potential for federal litigation that would result in the municipality paying not only for its own attorneys' fees (win or lose) but also the possibility of having to pay for the church's if the church should prevail. Therefore, RLUIPA's attorneys' fees provisions harm homeowners either by causing the church's interests to appear more valuable to the government than the neighbors' interests, or by creating an end result of higher property taxes paid by homeowners to cover all of the attorneys' fees.

When one takes these dynamics concerning attorneys' fees into account and then factors into the mix the fact that few ordinary residential homeowners can afford to be a participant in federal litigation, one can see how a church's ability to use RLUIPA against local governments has had the effect of disenfranchising homeowners from local land use processes. Congress has handed churches a club to be applied against homeowners and created financial incentives that further bury the homeowners' interests. Congress has apparently done all this without giving thought to the needs or interests of their millions of home-owning constituents.

The Psychic Cost of RLUIPA on Residential Homeowners

I have heard from one residential homeowner after another who was first bewildered by the invocation of RLUIPA when a church land use applicant threatened to sue the city at a public hearing, then angered by the unfairness of it, and then cowed by it. Homeowners are emotionally attached to their homes. This attachment is devalued by the policy behind RLUIPA, by the churches invoking RLUIPA, and often by the courts interpreting RLUIPA. It is now standard operating procedure for a religious entity demanding a variance, conditional use, or zoning change to charge any neighbors who deign to object to the zoning relief as "anti [fill in the applicant's religion]." This is usually when homeowners feel most violated because, given the demographics of the United States, they are most likely religious as well, and might even be a member of the denomination accusing them of bias.

It is impossible to count how many times residential homeowners have asked me what nonprofit organization would support their intent to fight RLUIPA in their case, or how many times I have had to tell them that no such organization exists. The churches have well-heeled groups, including the Becket Fund, the American Center for Law and Justice, the Rutherford Institute, the ACLU, and various law firms, among others, to champion their demands. Cities have organizations that will provide at least moral and informational support in the National League of Cities and the International

Municipal Lawyers Association. Yet no organization is devoted to supporting homeowners facing daunting odds in the land use process after RLUIPA is invoked, or to ensuring homeowners have a say in their own land use processes beyond the eminent domain arena, which is beyond RLUIPA's scope.

Congress's inattention to the concerns of homeowners under RLUIPA has left them feeling isolated and frustrated. Many would like to see Congress at the very least hold hearings to assess RLUIPA's impact on neighborhoods to make up for their analytical deficiencies the first time around. Once again, though, homeowners face difficult odds, because religious organizations have entrenched, well-practiced, and well-heeled lobbyists to represent their interests. In contrast, geographically dispersed, poorly financed homeowners must organize grassroots campaign in order to make their voices heard.

During RLPA and RLUIPA's pendency, in an attempt to mollify objectors, some members of Congress made promises to hold hearings on RLUIPA's impact after its enactment. The requirement was not written into the law and it has never happened. Justice and fairness demand that legislators rise above the interest group fray and weigh the interests of all of their constituents. Whether Congress can or will do this is yet to be seen.

Notes

1. To be sure, the Religious Freedom Restoration Act, invalidated in *City of Boerne v. Flores*, 521 U.S. 507, 511 (1997), is far worse on this score. Its formulation, which was nothing but a constitutional level of scrutiny, was the essence of opacity—nowhere in the law did it mention a single policy that would be affected by the statute—even though it affected every single law in the country.
2. There is no legislative history solely devoted to RLUIPA. Rather, the predecessor bill, the Religious Liberty Protection Act (RLPA), would have included land use law, and, therefore, hearings were held regarding RLPA and land use. It is to those hearings I am referring when I refer to "RLUIPA legislative history."
3. *Vill. of Belle Terre v. Boraas*, 416 U.S. 1, 9 (1974) (internal citation omitted).

4. As of 2006, the U.S. Census Bureau reported 68.8 million homeowners.
5. *Religious Liberty Protection Act of 1999: Hearing on H.R. 1691 Before the Subcomm. on the Constitution of the H. Comm. on the Judiciary*, 106th Cong. 287 (1999) (statement of Marci A. Hamilton, Professor of Law, Benjamin N. Cardozo School of Law).
6. *Religious Liberty Protection Act of 1998: Hearing on H.R. 4019 Before the Subcomm. on the Constitution of the H. Comm. on the Judiciary*, 105th Cong. 222 (1998) (statement of Marci A. Hamilton, Professor of Law, Benjamin N. Cardozo School of Law).
7. *See Kol Ami v. Abington Twp.*, 309 F.3d 120, 135 (2002) ("Indeed, land use law is one of the bastions of local control, largely free of federal intervention.").
8. 545 U.S. 469 (2005).
9. Charles Hurt, *Congress Assails Domain; Ruling Coalition Vows to Block Funds*, WASH. TIMES, July 1, 2005, at A01.
10. *League of Residential Neighborhood Advocates v. City of Los Angeles*, 498 F.3d 1052, 1057 (9th Cir. 2007) ("[T]he City impermissibly circumvented the procedural and substantive limitations contained in Los Angeles Municipal Code § 12.24. It granted the Congregation a right to use property in a residential neighborhood for congregational worship without going through the necessary procedures and issuing the requisite factual findings.").
11. In the interest of full disclosure, LRNA is one of my clients.
12. The Ninth Circuit discusses the lower court's unreported decision in *League of Residential Neighborhood Advocates v. City of Los Angeles,* 498 F.3d at 1054–1055.
13. *Id.* at 1058.
14. *Id.* (emphasis in original).
15. For that reason, I believe it violates the Constitution's inherent limits of federalism under *City of Boernes*, 521 U.S. 507 (1997), but that is beyond the topic of this chapter.
16. 544 U.S. 709 (1995).
17. *Castle Hills First Baptist Church v. City of Castle Hills*, 2004 WL 546792, at *11 (W.D. Tex. Mar. 17, 2004).
18. 42 U.S.C. § 1988(b).

5 RLUIPA—The Federal Perspective

Wendie L. Kellington

RLUIPA is a federal civil rights statute enacted to protect the free exercise of religion guaranteed by the First Amendment to the United States Constitution. It applies to institutionalized persons and in land use and land marking cases.[1] As with other federal civil rights statutes, RLUIPA authorizes the federal government to enforce its provisions.

The Civil Rights Division of the U.S. Department of Justice (DOJ) is charged with enforcing RLUIPA. The Civil Rights Division was established fifty years ago in response to profound racial discrimination. When the Civil Rights Act of 1957 became law, the position of Assistant Attorney General for Civil Rights was created within the DOJ, and the U.S. Commission on Civil Rights was created.[2]

Over the years, Congress has steadily increased the federal civil rights enforcement responsibilities of the Civil Rights Division. RLUIPA is the specific enforcement obligation of the DOJ's Housing and Civil Rights Enforcement Division, a subgroup of the Civil Rights Division. In 2002, the Civil Rights Division created and filled the position of "Special Counsel for Religious Discrimination" to coordinate the protection of religious liberties.[3] Before 2002, there was no comparable position in the DOJ.[4] The role of the Special Counsel is primarily to identify cases of religious discrimination and coordinate the federal enforcement response. RLUIPA is one tool available to resolve complaints of religious discrimination.

Three significant phenomena may account for the DOJ's higher profile in the protection of religious liberty. First, since the attacks of September 11, 2001, religious tensions in the United States have escalated.[5] Second, in the period between 1992 and 2005, complaints of religious discrimination in employment filed with the Equal Employment Opportunity Commission went up 69 percent.[6] This trend in religious discrimination is significantly disproportionate to other kinds of discrimination complaints filed in the same period. For example, in the same time frame, sex discrimination complaints increased by 6 percent, national origin discrimination complaints increased by 8 percent, and racial discrimination complaints decreased by nearly 10 percent.[7] Finally, Congress adopted specific findings in its enactment of RLUIPA acknowledging widespread discrimination against religious institutions by state and local officials in land use and land marking decisions. In adopting RLUIPA, "Congress recognized that places of assembly are required to facilitate religious practice, as well as the possibility that local governments may use zoning regulations to prevent religious groups from using land for such purposes."[8] It is not the province of the DOJ Civil Rights Division to second-guess congressional findings of profound discrimination.

Congress conducted nine hearings over a three-year period leading up to its adoption of RLUIPA and concluded that the record demonstrated a "widespread practice of individualized decisions to grant or refuse permission to use property for religious purposes," that these "individualized assessments readily lend themselves to discrimination," and that by their nature such assessments made it "difficult to prove discrimination in any individual case."[9] In other words, Congress believed there was significant opportunity for pretextual denials (denying free exercise of religious land use citing nonreligious bases). Accordingly, RLUIPA requires that decisions involving religious land uses be subjected to greater scrutiny than in traditional zoning cases where the "real" reason for denial of a religious land use may be masked.

The concern reflected in RLUIPA's adoption is not a new one; RLUIPA simply provides a specific mechanism to deter and stop pretextual denials and restrictions. In *American Friends of the Society of St. Pius, Inc. v. Schwab*, the court observed the efficacy of this approach:

> [H]uman experience teaches us that public officials, when faced with pressure to bar church uses by those residing in a residential neighborhood, tend to avoid any appearance of an antireligious stance and temper their decision by carefully couching their grounds [on some other basis].[10]

The concern that local elected officials may feel less allegiance to constitutional principles than to a vocal voting constituency is well established as adequate justification for federal intervention. In *West Virginia Board of Education v. Barnette*, the Court observed:

> [S]mall and local authority may feel less sense of responsibility to the Constitution and agencies of publicity may be less vigilant in calling it into account . . . .[11]

There can be no serious dispute that local discretionary land use decisions have a significant political aspect that furnishes a fertile basis for pretextual denial or impairment of the free exercise of religion.[12] In view of the significant congressional record of such denials and of the impairment of free exercise of religion in local land use and land marking processes, Congress acted to enforce the First Amendment using its Article V powers under the Fourteenth Amendment.

Given the significant bipartisan effort in its unanimous adoption of RLUIPA, it is not surprising that the DOJ vigorously enforces this statute. For the DOJ not to do so would lead to legitimate claims that the executive branch was ignoring what Congress (the legislative branch) set as the law and policy for the country.

RLUIPA has achieved its purposes due, in large measure, to the efforts of the federal government to enforce the statute. With significant assistance from the DOJ, RLUIPA has been used to overturn local zoning decisions, such as those excluding places of religious assembly from locations where private clubs and lodges were permitted, as a violation of RLUIPA's equal terms provisions.[13] RLUIPA has also been used to reverse local land use decisions found to impose a substantial burden on the free exercise of religion.[14]

Federal enforcement of RLUIPA occurs through (1) reviewing complaints and opening formal investigations, (2) filing litigation complaints specifically seeking RLUIPA enforcement and remedial measures, (3) intervening in RLUIPA litigation to support religious free exercise rights, and (4) supporting particular interpretations of RLUIPA in amicus briefs in selected cases. This multipronged approach is consistent with the Civil Rights Division's enforcement strategy: "(1) to fulfill the promise of federal laws entitling all persons to basic civil rights protections as they engage in everyday conduct throughout the United States; (2) to deter illegal conduct through the successful judicial enforcement of these federal laws; and (3) promoting voluntary compliance and civil rights protection through a variety of educational, technical assistance and outreach programs."[15]

On February 20, 2007, the DOJ launched a public information and education campaign regarding religious freedom, the First Freedom Project—a comprehensive federal effort to provide public information and service regarding the promotion and maintenance of religious liberty in the United States. The First Freedom project Web site (http://www.FirstFreedom.gov) contains information regarding regional seminars sponsored free of charge by DOJ officials about the agency's religious freedom law enforcement programs. A broad spectrum of other information is available, including reports on enforcement, information about various laws protecting religious freedom, and procedures by which aggrieved citizens can file complaints with the DOJ alleging violations of laws protecting religious liberty. The First Freedom Web site provides contact information and links to the DOJ Civil Rights Division. Another component of the First Freedom project is the Religious Liberty Task Force, which coordinates DOJ efforts to end religious discrimination in employment, housing, lending, public accommodation, and public facilities. The task force plays a role in the coordination of DOJ programs against bias crimes, and with respect to potential RLUIPA claims.

The DOJ's significant enforcement program for protecting religious liberty is designed to ensure that acts of religious intolerance are appropriately resolved, stopped, or, in some cases, punished. The twin parts of the program—education and enforcement—facilitate a national understanding of existing federal laws protecting religious liberty and commitment to enforcement.

The DOJ's efforts to protect religious freedom have been controversial because they are seen by critics as favoring religion. However, this criticism betrays a fundamental misunderstanding of the rationale for the First Amendment to the United States Constitution. The United States was the first government in recorded human history in which the leader was chosen by the people rather than by a divine power. Escaping the influence of the hereditary monarchy was a primary force in the creation of the government for the New World. An important corollary and equally fundamental premise for the formation of the United States was that citizens be allowed freedom of religious exercise, without prohibition or compulsion by the state. Constitutionally guaranteed religious freedom ensures a vigorous marketplace of religious ideas, making it impossible for one religious leader to claim a divine right to govern. This in turn helps to ensure the separation of church and state. The freedom to speak and believe as one chooses springs, in large measure, from the basic principle that there is no religious litmus test determining what one can believe or say. In *Everson v. Board of Education of Ewing Township*, the Supreme Court explained:

> A large proportion of the early settlers of this country came here from Europe to escape the bondage of laws which compelled them to support and attend government favored churches. The centuries immediately before and contemporaneous with the colonization of America had been filled with turmoil, civil strife, and persecutions, generated in large part by established sects determined to maintain their absolute political and religious supremacy. With the power of government supporting them, at various times and places, Catholics had persecuted Protestants, Protestants had persecuted Catholics, Protestant sects had persecuted other Protestant sects, Catholics of one shade of belief had persecuted Catholics of another shade of belief, and all of these had from time to time persecuted Jews. In efforts to force loyalty to whatever religious group happened to be

> on top and in league with the government of a particular time and place, men and women had been fined, cast in jail, cruelly tortured, and killed. Among the offenses for which these punishments had been inflicted were such things as speaking disrespectfully of the views of ministers of government-established churches, nonattendance at those churches, expressions of non-belief in their doctrines, and failure to pay taxes and tithes to support them.[16]

An indispensable corollary to these principles is the necessity for tolerance and freedom in the religious marketplace. This freedom requires a multiplicity of religious faiths, and state requirements on the numbers or types of faiths that might exist in a community are antithetical to this principle. Disguised religious litmus tests are as repugnant as overt ones. In *Lyng v. Northwest Indian Cemetery Protective Association*, the court cited *Federalist No. 10*, which "suggest[ed] that the effects of religious factionalism are best restrained through competition among a multiplicity of religious sects."[17] In the United States, churches of all faiths may be and are integrated within communities. No one church can dominate any other, and no church or faith can be prohibited, because of the guarantee of religious liberty. The geographic proximity of houses of worship to the homes of believers provides Americans with realistic opportunities for religious interaction and instruction of their choice.

In the context of the free exercise of religion, zoning restrictions have the unique potential to stifle or install religion. Such power can be overt, but it is more likely to be indirect. Indirect favoritism, extinguishment of particular faiths in a community, or the unavailability of competing faiths in a community can follow as an outgrowth of planning decisions regardless of whether they are aimed at manifesting such consequences, hence the role of RLUIPA in our constitutional form of government. In a June 21, 2007, written statement to the Committee on the Judiciary of the United States Senate, a former assistant attorney general in the Civil Rights Division, Wan J. Kim, explained in detail the activities that the DOJ had undertaken to enforce and protect religious liberty.[18] This statement explains that, as of its writing, the DOJ Civil Rights Division had enforced RLUIPA by reviewing more than 130 complaints, opening thirty formal investigations that were "resolved favorably without filing suit" involving "Muslims, Sikhs, Buddhists, Jews, Hindus, and Christians of various denominations"; by filing four RLUIPA lawsuits, and by filing amicus briefs on particular RLUIPA issues.[19]

In filing enforcement litigation against allegedly noncompliant local governments, the Housing and Civil Rights Enforcement Division has focused on cases on behalf of small and minority religious groups. One example is *United States v. City of Hollywood, Florida,* filed in April 2005, in which the Division filed a complaint alleging that certain land use actions with respect to a Jewish synagogue were discriminatory and violated RLUIPA's equal terms requirements.[20] This enforcement case led to a July 2006 consent decree in the District Court for the Southern District of Florida, containing three important and distinct elements. First, it allowed the particular religious land use to continue. Second, it established protective procedures for the local government to apply in subsequent religious free exercise cases and for RLUIPA/religious freedom training for local officials. Third, it provided for notice to citizens regarding free exercise rights and how to contact the DOJ Housing and Civil Rights Enforcement Division with concerns.[21] This consent decree is comprehensive and, as such, might provide a useful "safe harbor" template for appropriate local processing of land use cases involving religious free exercise.

The DOJ has also selected several cases in which to intervene on the side of the religious land use claimant or file amicus briefs regarding the proper interpretation of RLUIPA. While the DOJ has staked a position in a wide variety of RLUIPA cases, those implicating particular issues are more likely than others to attract federal attention. Challenges to RLUIPA's constitutionality or the related issue of the ripeness of the RLUIPA claim are likely to draw DOJ participation as amicus or as intervenor.

Likewise, there are particular kinds of RLUIPA issues that appear more likely than others to warrant the interest of the DOJ's enforcement arm. Local restrictions that appear to specifically target religious land uses, but do not apply to similar types of association land uses such as community centers and fraternal halls, often trigger federal investigation or litigation.[22]

The DOJ participated in *Midrash Sephardi, Inc. v. Town of Surfside*, in which the Eleventh Circuit determined that the town violated RLUIPA's equal terms provisions by allowing assembly uses but not religious assemblies.[23] Similarly, the DOJ brought a case against Maui County in *United States v. Maui County*, arguing that the county's denial of a church for reasons that were not similarly applied to similar association uses violated RLUIPA's equal terms provisions.[24] Allegations of religious discrimination are also likely to draw federal attention.[25] The DOJ has also been involved in cases where the interpretation of RLUIPA was important to the integrity of the statute, such as the test for measuring whether a "substantial burden" is imposed.[26]

An example of an issue that the federal government may find worthy of its attention and involvement concerns the juxtaposition of RLUIPA's "substantial burden" prong and the "total exclusion" prong. There is concern among religious entities and their advocates that interpreting the "substantial burden" provisions of RLUIPA to require proof that a religious land use is totally excluded from a locality, as some federal courts have, improperly merges the "substantial burden" prong of RLUIPA with the separate statutory requirement that a jurisdiction not totally exclude religious entities.[27]

Finally, federal involvement is likely to occur in cases that might establish useful RLUIPA precedent. Such decisional templates may provide helpful guidance to local governments on how to make land use decisions that comply with RLUIPA. Due in part to the DOJ's urging, the federal district court in *Castle Hills First Baptist Church v. City of Castle Hills* strongly encouraged local compliance with RLUIPA:

> The Court takes this opportunity to encourage Castle Hills and all other similarly situated communities to engage in thorough and positive debate and negotiation on the issues of zoning of religious organizations and places of worship, recognizing that in the arena of religion, all parties need trod lightly, out of respect for the beliefs of the adherents and out of respect for the importance of religion to our larger American culture. Cities must govern the health, safety and welfare of their communities, but in so doing, should consider carefully the positive and supportive role that a place of worship will play in doing so.[28]

Federal RLUIPA enforcement is not limited to litigation. In some instances, particularly in cases where a zoning ordinance demands restrictions on religious land uses that do not apply to similarly situated nonreligious land uses, the DOJ will open an investigation and the matter will be resolved without the need for litigation. As of June 21, 2007, there were thirty investigations opened and resolved, at least some of which involved this type of RLUIPA issue.[29]

As RLUIPA is a fairly new statute, the type of continued vigorous federal involvement seen in the past five years can be expected as part of the effort to ensure RLUIPA's ability to achieve its remedial purposes. It is likely that the U.S. Supreme Court will eventually take one of the many RLUIPA land use appeals and settle some of the questions that currently generate significant litigation and DOJ interest, such as whether or not RLUIPA is constitutional in the land use context, or the relationship between the substantial burden and exclusion prongs of the statute.

Further, as RLUIPA matures and more lower court decisions and consent decrees are issued, it is likely that federal involvement will be less necessary and less evident. As with school desegregation, the proportion of local government units that are appropriately self restrained in dealing with land use applications implicating religious free exercise rights will probably increase. Conversely, it is likely that religious institutions will better understand the limited reach of RLUIPA in local land use disputes and use the statute more sparingly and for its intended purposes. However, for the foreseeable future, unless RLUIPA is repealed, tenacious federal involvement can be expected to continue particularly in those cases involving (1) constitutional challenges to RLUIPA, (2) apparent facial RLUIPA "equal terms" violations, (3) interpretive issues that arguably merge RLUIPA's "substantial burden" provisions with its "total exclusion" prohibition, and (4) claims of pretextual religious discrimination.

Notes

1. *Guru Nanak Sikh Soc'y of Yuba City v. County of Sutter*, 456 F.3d 978, 985 (D. Haw. 2006).

2. Off. Att'y Gen., Order Regarding the Establishment of the Civil Rights Division, No. 155-57 (Dec. 9, 1957).
3. *See Changing Tides: Exploring the Current State of Civil Rights Enforcement: Hearing Before the Subcomm. on the Constitution of the H. Comm. on the Judiciary*, 110th Cong., 1st Sess. 2 (2007) (statement of Wan J. Kim, assistant attorney general, Civil Rights Division).
4. *Id.*
5. *See* DEPARTMENT OF JUSTICE, REPORT ON ENFORCEMENT OF LAWS PROTECTING RELIGIOUS FREEDOM: FISCAL YEARS 2001–06, at 4; *see also supra* note 3, at 3.
6. DEPARTMENT OF JUSTICE, *supra* note 5, at 4.
7. *Id.*
8. *Midrash Sephardi, Inc. v. Town of Surfside*, 366 F.3d 1214 (11th Cir. 2004), *cert. denied*, 125 S. Ct. 1295 (2005).
9. 146 CONG. REC. S7774 (daily ed. July 27, 2000).
10. 17 N.Y.S.2d 991, 993 (App. Div. 1979).
11. 319 U.S. 624, 637 (1943).
12. *See Cottonwood Christian Ctr. v. Cypress Redevelopment Agency*, 218 F. Supp. 2d 1203 (C.D. Cal. 2002).
13. *See Midrash Sephardi, Inc.*, 366 F.3d 1214 (11th Cir. 2004).
14. *Guru Nanak Sikh Soc'y of Yuba City v. County of Sutter*, 456 F.3d 978, 988-89 (9th Cir. 2006); *Sts. Constantine & Helen Greek Orthodox Church, Inc. v. City of New Berlin*, 396 F.3d 895, 899–900 (7th Cir. 2005).
15. U.S. Department of Justice, FY 2008 Performance Budget, Civil Rights Division, Congressional Budget Submission, http://www.usdoj.gov/jmd/2008justification/pdf/18_crt.pdf.
16. 330 U.S. 1, 9, *reh'g denied,* 330 U.S. 855 (1947).
17. 485 U.S. 439, 452 (1988). *Federalist No. 10* reads thus: "A religious sect may degenerate into a political faction in a part of the Confederacy; but the variety of sects dispersed over the entire face of it must secure the national councils against any danger from that source. A rage for paper money, for an abolition of debts, for an equal division of property, or for any other improper or wicked project, will be less apt to pervade the whole body of the Union than a particular member of it, in the same proportion as such a malady is more likely to taint a

particular county or district, than an entire State." The Federalist No. 10, at 128 (James Madison) (Isaac Kramnick ed., 1987).

18. *See supra* note 3.
19. *Id.*
20. No. 04-61212/05-60687 (S.D. Fla. filed Apr. 2005).
21. This consent decree can be viewed at http://www.usdoj.gov/crt/housing/documents/hollywoodsettle.pdf. Information about this case can be viewed on the First Freedom Web site.
22. *See Rocky Mountain Christian Church v. Bd. of County Comm'rs of Boulder*, 481 F. Supp. 2d 1213 (D. Colo. 2007) (intervenor on RLUIPA claim's ripeness and case merits); *Guru Nanak Sikh Soc'y of Yuba City v. County of Sutter*, 456 F.3d at 985 (intervenor and amicus briefing both the case merits and RLUIPA constitutionality); *Murphy v. New Milford Zoning Comm'n*, 402 F.3d 342 (2d Cir. 2005) (intervenor on RLUIPA constitutionality and ripeness); *Open Homes Fellowship, Inc. v. Orange County, Fla.*, 325 F. Supp. 2d 1349 (M.D. Fla. 2004) (intervention limited to defending RLUIPA's constitutionality); *Corp. of Presiding Bishop of Church of Jesus Christ of Latter-Day Saints v. City of West Linn*, 192 Or. App. 567, 570 (2004) (intervention limited to defending RLUIPA's constitutionality); *Civil Liberties for Urban Believers v. City of Chicago*, 342 F.3d 752 (7th Cir. 2003) (intervention limited to defending RLUIPA's constitutionality).
23. 366 F.3d 1214 (11th Cir. 2004), *cert. denied,* 125 S. Ct. 1295 (2005).
24. 298 F. Supp. 2d 1010 (D. Haw. 2003). *See also Lighthouse Inst. for Evangelism Inc. v. City of Long Branch*, 100 Fed. Appx. 70 (3d Cir. 2004) (unreported), *cert. denied,* 543 U.S. 1120 (2005) (DOJ intervention alleging violation of RLUIPA's equal terms provisions).
25. *See Hollywood Cmty. Synagogue, Inc. v. City of Hollywood, Fla.*, 436 F. Supp. 2d 1325, 1329–30 (S.D. Fla. 2006) (DOJ complaint sought injunctive and declaratory relief against city for violations of RLUIPA, 42 U.S.C.A. § 2000cc(b)(1)–(2), based on the city's treatment of religious organization on less than equal terms with nonreligious assemblies and on discrimination based on religion or religious denomination).
26. *See Sts. Constantine & Helen Greek Orthodox Church, Inc. v. City of New Berlin*, 396 F.3d 895, 899–900 (7th Cir. 2005); *Westchester*

Day Sch. v. Vill. of Mamaroneck, 386 F.3d 183, 189–90 (2d Cir. 2004).

27. *See Midrash Sephardi, Inc.*, 366 F.3d at 1127, and *Guru Nanak Sikh Soc'y v. County of Sutter*, 326 F. Supp. 2d 1140, 1153–54 (E.D. Cal. 2003), *aff'd,* 456 F.3d 978 (9th Cir. 2006) (determining that interpreting the term "substantial burden" to require a showing of total exclusion from the jurisdiction "would inappropriately fuse the 'substantial burden' prong of RLUIPA with the narrower 'exclusion limitation' provision"); *compare Civil Liberties for Urban Believers v. City of Chicago*, 342 F.3d 752 (determining in the context of a facial challenge to a city zoning ordinance that no RLUIPA substantial burden can be shown unless it is "effectively impracticable" for the religious land use to occur in the city).
28. *Castle Hills First Baptist Church v. City of Castle Hills*, 2004 WL 546792, at *20 (W.D. Tex. 2004).
29. *See supra* note 3.

RLUIPA in the Courts

Michael S. Giaimo

6

After nearly eight years of RLUIPA land use litigation in the federal district, appellate, and state courts, a body of case law has evolved that provides considerable guidance for practitioners in this field.[1] While a number of state court decisions are noteworthy, this chapter focuses on the most significant RLUIPA opinions thus far from the federal courts, with the understanding that this area of the law continues to evolve.[2]

Scope of Application

Land Use Regulation

RLUIPA applies by its terms to "land use regulation," which is in turn defined as "a zoning or landmarking law that limits claimants' use or development of land."[3] But courts have been faced with claims based on government actions concerning land that would not qualify as "zoning" or "landmarking" in their narrowest sense. Among other examples in this regard, the Ninth Circuit has assumed, without a formal decision, that the California Environmental Quality Act is a "land use regulation" subject to RLUIPA.[4] The federal district court in Hawaii has determined that Hawaii's statutory land classification scheme comes within the scope of the statute.[5] On the other hand, the Sixth Circuit rejected a plaintiff's attempt to apply the statute to the City's development of a road through church-owned property.[6] Similarly, the Third Circuit did not consider an ordinance requiring sewer tie in and payment of the associated fee to be "zoning" or "landmarking," and upheld the dismissal of a RLUIPA claim on that basis.[7] The Seventh Circuit has concluded that the annexation of land is neither zoning nor landmarking, and therefore not subject to RLUIPA.[8] A federal district court in California was willing to consider an eminent domain taking to prevent blight to be a "land use regulation" within the meaning of RLUIPA because the determination of blight was itself premised on an underlying zoning scheme; however, other courts have disagreed with this approach.[9]

Religious Exercise

The "substantial burden" provisions of RLUIPA apply with respect to "religious exercise," which is broadly defined by the statute as "any exercise of religion, whether or not compelled by or central to a system of religious belief."[10] Religious exercise protected by the statute specifically encompasses "the use, building, or conversion of real property for the purpose of religious exercise."[11] In addition to claims concerning approvals for the construction of a church or temple itself,[12] courts have considered that claims with respect to home worship,[13] religiously affiliated schools and colleges,[14] the construction of a parish center housing church-related offices and functions,[15] a residential drug and alcohol rehabilitation program,[16] and even a commercial wedding business[17] fall within RLUIPA's scope.

Although the definition of "religious exercise" in the statute is broad, it is not limitless. Not all activity conducted by a religious institution is protected. For example, in *Grace United Methodist Church v. City of Cheyenne* (2006),[18] the jury considered the question whether the operation of a day care center was religious exercise, and determined that it was not. The Tenth Circuit Court of Appeals concluded that the jury had been wrongly instructed in being asked to decide whether operating the day care center was an activity *fundamental* to the plaintiff's religious beliefs. However, the jury had separately found that the church did not prove that the operation of a day care center was a *sincere* exercise of its religious beliefs. Therefore, the error in the instruction was harmless.

In another case, the Second Circuit expressed doubt that RLUIPA's protection for religious exercise would extend to improvements at a religiously affiliated school if the improvements would be for exclusively secular use, such as a headmaster's residence or a gymnasium used only for sports.[19]

Substantial Burden

Many of the cases involve the question of what constitutes a "substantial burden." RLUIPA does not define the term "substantial burden," but the legislative history indicates that Congress did not intend to expand the operative test as articulated by the Supreme Court for claims under the First Amendment.[20] The plaintiff bears the burden of persuading the court that a "substantial burden" exists. As discussed below, some courts seem to have blurred the line between the "substantial burden" inquiry and the analytically separate question of whether a "substantial burden," once found, can be justified as furthering a compelling governmental interest by the least restrictive means. The following section discusses some of the leading cases addressing what constitutes a "substantial burden" under RLUIPA and notes the different formulations the various circuit courts have applied in this regard.

Lack of Alternate Sites and Difficulty of Approval Process

The question often arises whether difficulty in finding suitable alternative sites for religious worship or another protected form of religious exercise constitutes, in and of itself, a "substantial burden" imposed by the denial of a land use application or enforcement of a restrictive zoning provision. Similarly, plaintiffs often insist that the land use permitting process itself is so burdensome, as a matter of time, expense, or anticipated outcome, that it violates RLUIPA. These issues were both addressed in a frequently cited decision of the Court of Appeals for the Seventh Circuit, referred to as the *C.L.U.B.* case.[21]

In that case, an association of Chicago area churches and five individual churches challenged the city's zoning scheme under RLUIPA. They contended that a scarcity of available land where churches are allowed by right, combined with the complications, cost, difficulty, and political aspects of the special use permit process, imposed a "substantial burden" on the exercise of religion. The court held that such conditions "which are incidental to any high density urban land use" do not impose a "substantial burden" on religious exercise.[22] It defined "substantial burden" in the context of land use as a regulation "that necessarily bears direct, primary, and fundamental responsibility for rendering religious exercise—including the use of real property for the purpose thereof within the regulated jurisdiction generally—effectively impracticable."[23]

In another frequently cited case, *San Jose Christian College v. City of Morgan Hill* (2004), the Ninth Circuit considered whether a "substantial burden" resulted when a religiously affiliated college was denied the right to rezone a former hospital campus for its educational use. After defining a "substantial burden" as the imposition of "a significantly great restriction or onus upon" religious exercise, the court upheld summary judgment for the city, where the denial of the rezoning request was based on the college's refusal to submit a complete application and where, moreover, the college had not demonstrated that it was precluded from using other sites in the city.[24]

To similar effect, the plaintiff in *Petra Presbyterian Church v. Village of Northbrook* (2007) did not suffer a "substantial burden" just because churches were forbidden in the industrial zone. The plaintiff knew of the prohibition when it purchased its property in that zone, and it had neither presented evidence that land was unavailable in other zones where churches were allowed, nor evidence as to the difficulty of permitting in those other zones.[25] Likewise, in *Lighthouse Institute for Evangelism v. City of Long Branch* (*Lighthouse I*) (2004), the Third Circuit found no "substantial burden" where a church, which had been informed by the city that it would need a variance in order to construct a church on its newly purchased property, had already operated for many years under a lease at a nearby site, and also could have operated by right elsewhere in the city.[26]

The Eleventh Circuit Court of Appeals has formulated the following test:

> [A] "substantial" burden must place more than an inconvenience on religious exercise; a "substantial burden"

> is akin to significant pressure which directly coerces the religious adherent to conform his or her behavior accordingly. Thus, a "substantial burden" can result from pressure that tends to force adherents to forego religious precepts or from pressure that mandates religious conduct.[27]

Applying that test, the court in *Midrash Sephardi, Inc. v. Town of Surfside* (2004) ruled that the burden to members of two Orthodox Jewish congregations of having to walk "a few extra blocks" to services was not a "substantial" burden within the meaning of RLUIPA.[28] The difficulty the congregations would face in finding suitable land or facilities in a zoning district where religious uses were allowed as a conditional use was likewise not a "substantial burden," nor was having to seek a conditional use permit to locate there.

In another Eleventh Circuit case, *Konikov v. Orange County* (2005), the plaintiff, who was a rabbi, conducted Friday night and Saturday services at his home in a residentially zoned neighborhood.[29] The county took enforcement action on the grounds that a special exception was required to operate a "religious organization" in a residential zone. The plaintiff had never applied for a special exception but instead argued that there were private covenants encumbering his property that forbade him from doing so. The Eleventh Circuit concluded that having to file for a special exception "does not coerce conformity of a religious adherent's behavior" and therefore does not result in a "substantial burden."[30] It noted that the private covenants themselves might offend RLUIPA, but that the plaintiff had not presented such an argument.[31]

The Ninth Circuit in *Guru Nanak Sikh Society of Yuba City v. Sutter County* (2006) held that there was a "substantial burden" on the plaintiff's religious exercise in a case in which a Sikh group was denied permission to build a temple, even though there were other sites that might have been available.[32] The group first proposed to build on a 1.9-acre parcel in a residential area. Despite a favorable staff recommendation, the planning commission voted to deny the application based on fears that the noise and traffic would disrupt the surrounding neighborhood. The group then acquired a 28.8-acre parcel in an agricultural zone and proposed a temple on that site. After the planning commission approved the new application, neighbors appealed, and the Sutter County Board of Supervisors overturned the approval.[33]

In determining that the county had substantially burdened the religious group, the court observed that not every denial of a land use approval for a new worship facility necessarily constitutes a "substantial burden." However, in this case, the applicant had "readily agreed to every mitigation measure suggested by [planning staff] but the County, without explanation, found such cooperation insufficient," and the court felt that the reasons for the denial "could easily be applied to all future applications" by the group.[34] This "to a significantly great extent lessened the possibility that future . . . applications would be successful," resulting in a "substantial burden," as the court saw it.[35] The court also found that in previously approving an application by another Sikh group to locate a temple on similar agricultural land but denying the plaintiff the right to do so because of concerns about "leapfrog development," the county had been inconsistent in how it applied its standards to church projects, meaning that any future application would be "fraught with uncertainty."[36] The court refused to credit the county's assurance in the second denial that it would cooperate with the applicant to find a suitable site. Although "the availability of other suitable property weighs against the finding of a 'substantial burden' . . . RLUIPA does not contemplate that local governments can use broad and discretionary land use rationales as leverage to select the precise parcel of land where a religious group can worship."[37]

Following, but seeming to go beyond, the *Guru Nanak* approach, the *Westchester Day School* case in the Second Circuit provides a good illustration of how the "substantial burden" inquiry is not only highly dependent on fact, but also how, in practice, it can be colored by contextual factors. In that case, the plaintiff, a religiously affiliated grade school, sought to amend its special permit to build a new building, renovate existing classrooms, and add parking to its campus. After initially determining that the school would not be required to conduct an environmental impact evaluation of the expansion, when faced with community opposition the local zoning board reversed itself. The school then sued under RLUIPA and state law, and the case embarked on a protracted procedural course.[38]

Eventually, the Second Circuit, which had earlier vacated summary judgment in favor of the plaintiff and remanded for trial, reviewed the case for a second time. The court first confirmed the district court's finding that the renovated classrooms and other improvements would be "used for religious education and practice," and therefore the project was a protected "religious exercise" under RLUIPA.[39] It then considered whether the denial of the application substantially burdened the plaintiff's religious exercise. Following the Eleventh Circuit's focus on whether the burden would force the religious adherent to change behavior, the court stated that "if there is a reasonable opportunity for the institution to submit a modified application, the denial does not place substantial pressure on it to change its behavior and thus does not constitute a 'substantial burden' on the free exercise of religion."[40] However, it cautioned that "a conditional denial may represent a 'substantial burden' if the condition itself is a burden on free exercise, the required modifications are economically unfeasible, or where a zoning board's stated willingness to consider a modified plan is disingenuous."[41]

Having already observed that "the neutral application of legitimate land use restrictions" would rarely support a "substantial burden" claim, the court noted the district court's finding that the denial of the school's application was "arbitrary and capricious" under state law because the rationale for the decision was not within the police power and was not justified by substantial evidence.[42] But rather than taking up this concern as part of a later inquiry into whether there was a "compelling governmental interest" for a denial, assuming that the denial otherwise imposed a "substantial burden," the court treated this lack of proper justification itself as grounds for placing a thumb on the "substantial burden" scale. The court also asked whether there were "quick, reliable, and financially feasible alternatives" available to the plaintiff, such as reallocating space in existing buildings, and whether the denial was conditional, such that the plaintiff would have an opportunity to submit a revised proposal to address the zoning board's concerns or whether, instead, it was "absolute."[43] Finding that the board could have imposed conditions based on health, safety, and welfare but did not; that the board members discarded their notes after the hearing, thereby suggesting that they considered the decision to be "final"; that it would be economically unduly burdensome for the plaintiff to submit a new application; and that the board members were not credible in saying they would be willing to consider a new application, the court upheld the district court in ordering that a special permit issue for the proposed expansion.[44]

It is plain to see that the *Westchester Day School* court, like the Ninth Circuit in *Guru Nanak*, felt that the plaintiff had been poorly treated by the board, and it is plain to understand the outcome of the case in that respect. It is less easy to credit the rigor of the approach this case takes to the "substantial burden" inquiry, or its value as precedent in that regard.[45]

Conditions of Approval

The Court of Appeals for the Sixth Circuit, in *Living Water Church of God v. Charter Township of Meridian* (2007), framed the "substantial burden" inquiry as follows: "Though the government action may make religious exercise more expensive or difficult, does the government action place substantial pressure on a religious institution to violate its religious beliefs or effectively bar a religious institution from using its property in the exercise of its religion?"[46] Using that rubric, the court held that even though limits were placed on the size to which an existing church could expand, resulting in expense and delay that posed an inconvenience to the plaintiff, which could not build its "ideal" facility, there was no "substantial burden" under RLUIPA. The plaintiff had not demonstrated that it could not carry out its "missions and ministries" within the existing facility or one that was expanded to a permissible extent.[47] In another Sixth Circuit decision, *DiLaura v. Ann Arbor Charter Twp.* (2002), the issuance of a bed-and-breakfast permit did not moot a pending RLUIPA claim by plaintiffs looking to start a retreat house, because the regulatory limitations on such a permit would require payment by guests, would have limited the service of communion wine, and would have prevented serving dinner to overnight guests, all of which the court found to impose a "substantial burden" on religious exercise.[48]

In *Vision Church v. Village of Long Grove* (2007), the Seventh Circuit held that the denial of a voluntary annexation petition and later denial of a special use permit to construct a church did not impose a "substantial burden" on the plaintiff religious corporation.[49] After initially proposing construction of a 99,000-square-foot facility, the plaintiff reduced the proposed size to 56,200 square feet and entered into negotiations with the village over the conditions of annexation. The plaintiff agreed to some terms but refused to accept those that would have prevented additional parking areas and buildings, precluded the construction of a ball field in a particular area, and limited the number of Sunday services and "major events" during the week. Accordingly, the village denied the petition.[50] Later, after the property was involuntarily annexed, the plaintiff again proposed a 99,000-square-foot facility in the face of a pending ordinance that would have restricted the size of assembly buildings to 55,000 square feet.[51] The ordinance passed, and the village denied a special use application for the larger facility. The church sued on multiple grounds, including a "substantial burden" claim. Although the Seventh Circuit found the attempt to regulate activities at the church "troublesome," it concluded that none of the rejected conditions would have imposed a "substantial burden" under its *C.L.U.B.* formulation.[52] Citing *Midrash Sephardi* with approval, it held that "a burden must be more than a mere inconvenience to rise to the level of a constitutional injury; it must place significant pressure on [the church] to forego religious precepts or to engage in religious conduct."[53] The court also found, based on the record, that there likely would have been a church constructed had the plaintiff been willing to construct a 55,000-square-foot facility to satisfy the assembly ordinance, and that such a facility would have been more than ample to meet the size of the current church congregation and accommodate even eightfold growth.[54]

To similar pragmatic effect, but with the opposite outcome, the Seventh Circuit had earlier decided *Saints Constantine and Helen Greek Orthodox Church, Inc. v. City of New Berlin* (2005).[55] In that case, a religious group sought to rezone its parcel of residentially zoned land to an institutional classification so it could build a church under a planned unit development (PUD). The planning commission voiced concern about the effect of the rezoning if the group were to sell the property, and denied the request. It suggested that the group instead apply for a conditional use permit to construct the church in the residential zone, but the church demurred because under that approach it would be unable to raise funds in time to start construction before the permit lapsed.[56] The city later suggested that the church seek a PUD while retaining the residential zoning, an approach that the Seventh Circuit concluded was the legal and functional equivalent of the approach proposed by the church but earlier rejected by the planning commission.[57] The district court had held, following *C.L.U.B.*, that the church could not demonstrate a "substantial burden" from the denial of the rezoning unless it also demonstrated that there was no other property on which to build the church. Backing away from the "effectively impracticable" standard of *C.L.U.B.*, the Seventh Circuit reversed, finding that the plaintiff faced a "burden" that was "substantial" in the form of "delay, uncertainty, and expense," whether it had to look for another property on the one hand, or had to continue to file applications on the other.[58] Noting the "whiff of bad faith" arising from the city's initial rejection of an approach that appeared to be the same as the one it later offered as a solution, the court remanded with direction that the entry of judgment against the city be stayed for ninety days to allow the parties to devise a way to address the city's concern that the property not end up in nonreligious institutional use.[59] Like the *Westchester Day School* and *Guru Nanak* cases, the "substantial burden" analysis in this case appears to have been colored by a sense of unfair or inept treatment by the local land use boards.

Compelling Governmental Interest/Least Restrictive Means

If a plaintiff demonstrates that a land use decision has imposed a "substantial burden" on its religious exercise, it is incumbent on the government to show that the burden is justified by a compelling governmental interest furthered through the least restrictive means. Courts have assumed that health and safety interests are compelling. One district court asserted that government interests in promoting consistency of land use, preserving open space, curbing noise, regulating traffic, facilitating public transportation, and preserving historic structures could be found compelling.[60] However blight and a desire to increase the tax base have been held, in at least one case, not to be compelling.[61]

The *Westchester Day School* case illustrates the principle that the compelling interest showing must be made with respect to the particular matter in question, and not just as a general assertion. In that case, the government claimed a compelling interest in protecting its residents' safety by controlling traffic and enforcing zoning regulations. But the court of appeals noted the district court's finding that the asserted reasons for the denial were pretext.[62] Moreover, even if the reasons were credited as "compelling," the court noted that the board could have issued an approval with conditions to mitigate the concerns, rather than deny the application altogether.[63]

In *Elsinore Christian Center v. City of Lake Elsinore* (2003), the city argued that the denial of a conditional use permit to allow a church to operate at a particular location furthered the interests of curbing urban blight and preserving the tax base, in that the current tenant of the location in question was a discount food store. The court found that even if those reasons could be assumed to be compelling governmental interests, the denial of the permit did not further those interests, because the evidence showed that the landlord intended to evict the food store regardless of whether the church moved in.[64]

Employing the "least restrictive means" to accomplish a compelling governmental objective does not necessarily require that the religious land use application be approved in some fashion. Even the denial of an application outright after careful consideration may suffice as the "least restrictive means" of furthering compelling governmental interests in the circumstance where an applicant refused to compromise on anything less than its preferred plan.[65]

Jurisdictional Prongs

The "substantial burden" provisions of RLUIPA apply under the following conditions:

1. The substantial burden is imposed in a program or activity that receives Federal financial assistance, even if the burden results from a rule of general applicability;
2. The substantial burden affects, or removal of that substantial burden would affect, commerce with foreign nations, among the several States, or with Indian

tribes, even if the burden results from a rule of general applicability; or

3. The substantial burden is imposed in the implementation of a land use regulation or system of land use regulations, under which a government makes, or has in place formal or informal procedures or practices that permit the government to make, individualized assessments of the proposed uses for the property involved.[66]

These jurisdictional limitations are intended to establish the constitutional underpinnings of RLUIPA's call for strict scrutiny review of "substantial burdens" on religious exercise. They are grounded, respectively, in Congress's power under the spending clause, its power under the commerce clause, and the parameters of free exercise clause jurisprudence.[67] To date, there is a dearth of land use cases under the federal financial assistance prong. However, commerce clause and individual assessment jurisdiction have been addressed on many occasions.

In cases concerning the construction of buildings, courts have not generally had difficulty finding that the Commerce Clause nexus has been satisfied on the basis of the construction activity alone.[68] A Commerce Clause nexus has also been upheld where it was assumed that guests of a retreat house might travel from other states, and in a case involving a church with a televised ministry and bookstore.[69]

The individualized assessments provision has been said to apply "when the government may take into account the particular details of an applicant's proposed use of land when deciding to permit or deny that use."[70] As such, it has been held or assumed to apply to all varieties of discretionary land use permitting processes.[71] However, on this basis there would not be jurisdiction for a facial challenge to a zoning classification that did not entail particular review of an individual's application.[72] Although the plain language and syntax of the statute would suggest otherwise, it has been argued that these jurisdictional provisions apply not only to the "substantial burden" requirements of subsection (a)(1) of RLUIPA, but also to the equal terms, nondiscrimination, and exclusion provisions of subsections (b)(1) through (3). Faced with such an argument, the Eleventh Circuit in *Midrash Sephardi* expressed doubt that the statutory language would support such a reading, but did not need to dispose of the question as the test would have been satisfied anyway under the facts of that case.[73]

Equal Terms

RLUIPA provides that "[n]o government shall impose or implement a land use regulation in a manner that treats a religious assembly or institution on less than equal terms with a nonreligious assembly or institution."[74] The Eleventh Circuit, in *Primera Iglesia Bautista Hispana of Boca Raton, Inc. v. Broward County* (2006), addressed the claim that a zoning provision requiring one thousand feet of separation between nonagricultural, nonresidential uses had a discriminatory effect on a proposed religious use.[75] The court identified what it termed "three distinct kinds" of equal terms violations:

> (1) a statute that facially differentiates between religious and nonreligious assemblies or institutions, (2) a facially neutral statute that is nevertheless "gerrymandered" to place a burden solely on religious, as opposed to nonreligious, assemblies or institutions, or (3) a truly neutral statute that is selectively enforced against religious, as opposed to nonreligious assemblies or institutions.[76]

The court noted that it had encountered the first type of violation in *Midrash Sephardi*, where a city allowed private clubs and lodges in the business district, but prohibited religious assemblies like churches and synagogues.[77] The *Midrash Sephardi* court concluded that private clubs and lodges were assemblies, and that a violation of the equal terms provision was disclosed by their more favorable treatment under the zoning code.[78] It made no difference that there actually were no private clubs or lodges in the city.[79] The violation was shown on the face of the code. The *Midrash Sephardi* court then applied "strict scrutiny" to the distinction in treatment, ultimately finding that it could not survive because it was not "narrowly tailored" to the government's proffered interest in promoting retail and service activities in the business district.[80] In *Vision Church*, by contrast, the Seventh Circuit rejected an equal terms argument founded on differences in treatment between plaintiff's religious use in a residential zone, and the restaurants and tea rooms permitted in a business district. It also rejected comparisons to elementary schools that were built before the plaintiff church at a time when different standards applied.[81]

The Primera Iglesia court explained that the second type of violation is exemplified by the animal sacrifice ordinance invalidated by the U.S. Supreme Court in *Lukumi*.[82] Although that ordinance was drafted in neutral terms, the Supreme Court found that it was intentionally calculated to target ritual slaughter with religious motivations, and to avoid interference with other practices entailing the killing of animals, such as the preparation of food. Focusing on the *Primera Iglesia* facts, the Eleventh Circuit concluded that the separation distance requirement applied generally to all nonagricultural and nonresidential uses, and that there were no special carve-outs for other nonreligious uses. Moreover, the provisions under which the church had tried, but failed twice, to obtain a variance from the separation requirement were "likewise neutral and generally applicable."[83] Further, there was no evidence that the plaintiffs had been the target of the requirement, which had been adopted before it acquired the land in question.[84]

The third type of violation concerns the selective application of a neutral requirement. The *Primera Iglesia* court considered the plaintiff's argument that, at about the same time it was denied a variance, a nearby school succeeded in having its property rezoned to a district where the separation requirement did not apply. It held that the school was not an apt comparison because, unlike the church, it had not requested a variance. The *Primera Iglesia* court contrasted the *Konikov* case where the plaintiff succeeded in demonstrating an "as applied" violation of the equal terms provision.[85] In that case, the zoning code required both religious and social organizations to obtain a special use permit to locate in a residential zone. Nonetheless, in determining whether to apply the permit requirement to a particular gathering, the city applied different standards to religious and nonreligious uses. As the *Konikov* court had observed:

> For example, a cub scout troop meeting held two to three times a week would not be a violation. Similarly, friends gathering to watch sports two to three times weekly would

> not violate the Code. If the assembly's purpose was to celebrate birthdays, holidays, or a simple family dinner, that would not constitute a violation. In other words, a group meeting with the same frequency as Konikov's would not violate the Code, *so long as religion is not discussed.*[86]

The Third Circuit subsequently held, in *Lighthouse Institute for Evangelism, Inc. v. City of Long Branch* (*Lighthouse II*) (2007), that the equal terms provision requires the plaintiff to do more than merely identify any nonreligious assembly or institution that would theoretically be treated more favorably under the regulation in question. The plaintiff church need not point to a secular use to which it is similar in all respects, but must at a minimum identify a secular use that is similarly situated with respect to the objectives of the regulation in question.[87] Having cut back on this aspect of the *Midrash* court's reading of the equal terms provisions, the Third Circuit then took the view that the *Midrash* court was also wrong in applying "strict scrutiny" to the equal terms provisions of the statute. Instead, if the plaintiff was able to demonstrate that a similarly situated secular use was more favorably treated under a land use requirement, the requirement in question could not be saved by finding that it survived a "strict scrutiny" calculus. Instead, the offending government would be strictly liable.[88] Ultimately, the court in *Lighthouse II* found that there was no nonreligious entity similarly situated to the plaintiff with respect to the city's objectives of creating a retail and entertainment district, because only religious uses would implicate a state statute that imposed a separation requirement between establishments with liquor licenses and churches.[89]

Nondiscrimination

RLUIPA forbids government from implementing "a land use regulation that discriminates against any assembly or institution on the basis of religion or religious denomination."[90] One plaintiff sought unsuccessfully to avail itself of this provision by arguing that its religiously motivated residential drug and alcohol rehabilitation program was regulated in a way that a residential religious study program would not have been. The Court found this analysis inapt, instead viewing the "apples to apples" comparison as whether a nonreligious rehabilitation facility would have been better treated.[91]

Exclusion

A jurisdiction may not totally exclude religious assemblies or unreasonably limit religious assemblies, institutions, or structures.[92] A claim under this provision requires more than simply demonstrating that a particular application has been denied for a particular proposal at a particular location.[93] The Seventh Circuit Court of Appeals in *Vision Church* evaluated a claim that the exercise of unbridled discretion in considering a special use permit application was "unreasonable" in violation of this provision. The court declined to take that view, noting that "[t]his is not a case where the state has delegated essentially standardless discretion to nonprofessionals operating without procedural safeguards."[94] Moreover, the court noted, "even if the Zoning Regulations were to grant the Board undue discretion," it would not demonstrate a violation of this provision because the "requirement that churches obtain a special use permit requirement is neutral on its face and is justified by legitimate, non-discriminatory municipal planning goals."[95]

Constitutionality

Several decisions have considered challenges to RLUIPA on a variety of constitutional grounds. Defendants have claimed, in light of the jurisdictional prerequisites for a "substantial burden" challenge, that the statute exceeds Congress's powers under section 5 of the Fourteenth Amendment, the Commerce Clause, and the Spending Clause. Defendants have claimed that the statute violates the Establishment Clause, that it violates the Tenth Amendment, and offends separation of power principles. Thus far, these cases have invariably concluded that the statute survives constitutional scrutiny in all respects.[96]

Only one reported decision to date has found the land use provisions of RLUIPA to be unconstitutional. That case, *Elsinore Christian Center v. City of Lake Elsinore* (2006), held that the "substantial burden" provisions exceeded Congress's authority under section 5 of the Fourteenth Amendment because, among other shortcomings, it "vastly expanded" the scope of religious exercise that received "strict scrutiny" protections.[97] It also concluded that Congress exceeded its authority under the Commerce Clause in applying the "substantial burden" provisions to the regulation of activity affecting interstate commerce.[98] This decision was later reversed by the Ninth Circuit.

To date, the only case to reach the U.S. Supreme Court on the question of RLUIPA's constitutionality is *Cutter v. Wilkinson*, which concerned a facial challenge to the prisoner's rights provisions of the statute on Establishment Clause grounds.[99] A unanimous court in *Cutter* held that the provisions in question were a permissible accommodation in that they alleviate government burdens on private religious exercise but do not elevate religion over the significant interests of maintaining order and security in a penal institution. The court explicitly noted that it was expressing no opinion as to the land use provisions of the statute, and invited future challenges on an "as applied" basis in the event that requests for religious accommodations threatened to overwhelm other institutional interests.[100]

Ripeness

Several cases have dealt with the issue of when a RLUIPA claim is ripe for adjudication. In one of the earliest reported RLUIPA cases, *Murphy v. New Milford Zoning Commission*, a couple who conducted private prayer meetings in their home challenged a local zoning enforcement order that would have prevented them from hosting "regularly scheduled" meetings with more than twenty-five non–family members as participants. The couple obtained a temporary injunction, later made permanent, to prevent enforcement of the order.[101] On appeal, however, the Second Circuit Court of Appeals applied the ripeness test set forth by the U.S. Supreme Court in *Williamson County Regional Planning Commission v. Hamilton Bank* (1985).[102] Under this test, before bringing a land use claim in federal court a property owner must first obtain a final, definitive ruling from the regulating entity as to how the regulations in question will be applied to its property. The plaintiffs had neither appealed the zoning enforcement order to the local zoning board of appeals, nor taken the opportunity to seek a zoning variance from that board. Therefore, the court dismissed the case.[103]

By contrast, the Eleventh Circuit had no problem finding the *Konikov* case ripe for disposition because the local code enforcement board had already determined that the plaintiff was in violation of zoning, based upon his use of his home for religious services, and imposed a fine for his failure to come into compliance. The imposition of the fine signaled that the local decision applying the code to the plaintiff was final and ripe for adjudication.[104]

The Sixth Circuit found the *DiLaura* case ripe for adjudication after the plaintiff had filed for and been denied a variance to start a retreat house even though the plaintiffs had not commenced the retreat house use and the township had not commenced enforcement proceedings. The court rejected the township's argument that it "might not enforce" its ordinance, finding that such a course would be "contrary to law," as enforcement would be mandatory, and there was the possibility of significant penalty for a violation.[105] In another case, a district court found a facial challenge to an ordinance to be ripe for adjudication under RLUIPA, where the plaintiff claimed that merely seeking an exception under the ordinance would impose a "substantial burden," and the court felt that the issues were sufficiently focused.[106]

Settlement

RLUIPA provides by its terms that "government may avoid the preemptive force of any provision of this chapter by changing the policy or practice that results in a substantial burden on religious exercise, by retaining the policy or practice and exempting the substantially burdened religious exercise, by providing exemptions from the policy or practice for applications that substantially burden religious exercise, or by any other means that eliminates the substantial burden."[107] Many cases, including some that have received substantial attention in the press, have been resolved by agreement, either before a disposition at the trial level or while on appeal. However, in *League of Residential Neighborhood Advocates v. City of Los Angeles* (2007), the Ninth Circuit held that a settlement agreement between a synagogue and the city in resolution of a RLUIPA claim was invalid under state law. The agreement approved the religious use of the property that would otherwise have entailed discretionary approval under local zoning processes.[108] The Ninth Circuit held that the court had no authority to allow the city to bargain away its police powers in the absence of a finding that federal law had been or would be violated. However, here the RLUIPA claim was contested by the city and the city had disclaimed any violation even in the settlement agreement itself.

Conclusion

The RLUIPA landscape is ever changing, as evidenced by the brief overview provided in this chapter. As consensus develops on certain issues, new ones emerge. Meanwhile, it seems inevitable that the U.S. Supreme Court will eventually address both the constitutionality of the statute's land use provisions and the interpretation of some of its more vexing provisions. Planners, municipal officials, land use attorneys, clergy, and others who are concerned with religious land use issues would be well advised to keep up with the latest case decisions in this area, both within their own jurisdictions and elsewhere.

Notes

1. Although it undoubtedly will before long, the United States Supreme Court has not, as of this writing, decided a RLUIPA land use case.
2. RLUIPA claims may be brought in either federal or state court. Noteworthy state court decisions interpreting RLUIPA include *Church of Latter-Day Saints v. City of West Linn,* 86 P.3d 1140 (Or. App. 2004), and *Greater Bible Way Temple v. City of Jackson,* 733 N.W.2d 734 (Mich. 2007).
3. 42 U.S.C. § 2000cc-5(5).
4. *San Jose Christian Coll. v. City of Morgan Hill*, 360 F.3d 1024, 1036 (9th Cir. 2004).

5. *Hale O Kaula Church v. Maui Planning Comm'n*, 229 F. Supp. 2d 1056 (D. Haw. 2002).
6. *Prater v. Burnside*, 289 F.3d 417 (6th Cir. 2002).
7. *Second Baptist Church v. Gilpin Twp.*, 118 Fed. Appx. 615, 617 (3d Cir. 2004).
8. *Vision Church v. Vill. of Long Grove*, 468 F.3d 975, 998 (7th Cir. 2006), *reh'g en banc denied*, 2007 U.S. App. LEXIS 639 (2007).
9. *Cottonwood Christian Ctr. v. Cypress Redevelopment Agency*, 218 F. Supp. 2d 1203, 1222 (D. Cal. 2002); *compare Faith Temple Church v. Town of Brighton*, 402 F. Supp. 2d 250, 256–58 (W.D.N.Y. 2005).
10. 42 U.S.C. § 2000cc-5(7)(A).
11. 42 U.S.C. § 2000cc-5(7)(B).
12. *See, e.g., Petra Presbyterian Church v. Vill. of Northbrook*, 489 F.3d 846 (7th Cir. 2007) (church); *Guru Nanak Sikh Soc'y of Yuba City v. Sutter County*, 456 F.3d 978 (9th Cir. 2006) (Sikh temple).
13. *Murphy v. Zoning Comm'n of the Town of New Milford*, 148 F. Supp. 2d 173 (D. Conn. 2001) (prayer group in a private home), *vacated*, 402 F.3d 342 (2d Cir. 2005); *Konikov v. Orange County*, 302 F. Supp. 2d 328 (M.D. Fla. 2004) (Jewish shul in a suburban residence); *DiLaura v. Ann Arbor Charter Twp*, 30 Fed. Appx. 501 (6th Cir. 2002) (use of private home for religious retreats).
14. *Westchester Day Sch. v. Vill. of Mamaroneck*, 504 F.3d 338 (2d Cir. 2007) [hereinafter *Westchester Day Sch. II*] (day school with a religious mission); *Shepherd Montessori Center Milan v. Ann Arbor Charter Twp.*, 259 Mich. App. 315 (2003) (faith-based primary school); *San Jose Christian Coll.*, 360 F.3d 1024 (religious college).
15. *Mintz v. Roman Catholic Bishop of Springfield*, 424 F. Supp. 2d 309 (D. Mass. 2006).
16. *Men of Destiny Ministries v. Osceola County*, 2006 WL 3219321 (M.D. Fla. 2006).
17. *Kaahumanu v. County of Maui*, 315 F.3d 1215 (9th Cir. 2003).
18. 451 F.3d 643 (10th Cir. 2006). *But see Living Water Church of God v. Charter Twp. of Meridian*, 258 Fed. Appx. 729, 733 (6th Cir. 2007) (considering plaintiff's "day care ministry" to be religious exercise).
19. *Westchester Day Sch. II*, 504 F.3d at 347–48.

20. 146 Cong. Rec. S7774, 7776 (daily ed. July 27, 2000) (joint statement of Sens. Hatch and Kennedy); *see, e.g.*, *Lyng v. Northwest Indian Cemetery Protective Ass'n*, 485 U.S. 439, 450–51 (1988) (government burden having a "tendency to coerce individuals into acting contrary to their religious beliefs"); *Thomas v. Review Bd. of Ind. Employment Sec. Div.*, 450 U.S. 707, 717–18 (1981) ("substantial pressure on an adherent to modify his behavior and to violate his beliefs").
21. *Civil Liberties for Urban Believers v. City of Chicago*, 342 F.3d 752 (7th Cir. 2003) [hereinafter *C.L.U.B.*].
22. *Id.* at 761.
23. *Id.*
24. *San Jose Christian Coll.*, 360 F.3d at 1034–36.
25. *Petra Presbyterian*, 489 F.3d at 851.
26. 100 Fed. Appx. 70 (3d Cir. 2004).
27. *Midrash Sephardi, Inc. v. Town of Surfside*, 366 F.3d 1214, 1227 (11th Cir. 2004).
28. *Id.*; *see also Episcopal Student Found. v. City of Ann Arbor*, 341 F. Supp. 2d 691 (W.D. Mich. 2004) (holding that "financial and logistical difficulties" were not sufficient to demonstrate "substantial burden").
29. *Konikov v. Orange County*, 410 F.3d 1317 (11th Cir. 2005).
30. *Id.* at 1323–24.
31. *Id.* at 1323.
32. *Guru Nanak Sikh Soc'y*, 456 F.3d 978.
33. *Id.* at 981–84.
34. *Id.* at 989.
35. *Id.*
36. *Id.* at 991.
37. *Id.* at 992 n.20.
38. *Westchester Day Sch. II*, 504 F.3d 338. The federal district court first concluded that the zoning board had wrongly rescinded its initial ruling. The zoning board then conducted hearings on the merits and denied the special permit application. The plaintiff then amended its complaint to challenge this denial under RLUIPA. The district court granted partial summary judgment for the plaintiff, and the Second Circuit reversed and remanded for further proceedings. A bench trial was then held, at which the court also ruled in the plaintiff's favor, and the Second Circuit got the

case for the second time. The Second Circuit finally upheld the district court's order that the permit issue, six years after the initial zoning application was filed.

39. *Id.* at 348.
40. *Id.* at 349.
41. *Id.* (citing *Westchester Day Sch. v. Vill. of Mamaroneck,* 386 F.3d 183, 188 (2d Cir. 2004)).
42. 504 F.3d at 351.
43. *Id.* at 352.
44. *Id.* at 352–53, 357.
45. One might also view *Westchester Day Sch. II* as implicitly reducing the threshold for measuring "substantial burden" in a situation where an expansion of a long-standing religious use is proposed and therefore considering alternative sites is thought in and of itself to create a "substantial burden." *See, e.g., Mintz,* 424 F. Supp. 2d 309 (court notes that church has existed at the same site for ninety years and rejects suggestion that parish center could be established at a different location).
46. 258 Fed. Appx. at 737.
47. *Id.* at 741.
48. 112 Fed. Appx. 445, 446 (6th Cir. 2004).
49. 468 F.3d at 998–99.
50. *Id.* at 982–83.
51. *Id.* at 983–84.
52. *Id.* at 999.
53. *Id.* (internal quotations omitted).
54. *Id.* at 999–1000.
55. 396 F.3d 895 (7th Cir.), *reh'g en banc denied,* 2005 U.S. App. LEXIS 3991 (2005).
56. 396 F.3d at 898–99.
57. *Id.* at 899.
58. *Id.* at 899–901.
59. *Id.* at 901; *see also Grace Church of N. County v. City of San Diego,* 555 F. Supp. 2d 1126, 1136 (S.D. Cal. 2008) (uncertainty and financial risk created when city issued conditional use permit to church for a term that was only half the duration of its lease constituted "substantial burden").
60. *Redwood Christian Schs. v. County of Alameda,* 2007 U.S. Dist. LEXIS 53165, at *9 (N.D. Cal. 2007); *see also Mintz,* 424 F. Supp. 2d

at 324 (rejecting argument that town had compelling interest in 200-foot setback and 4 percent lot coverage requirements for religious institutions, but assuming *arguendo* that traffic and parking interests could be compelling). *But see Mount St. Scholastica, Inc. v. City of Atchison*, 482 F. Supp. 2d 1281, 1285 (D. Kan. 2007) (asserting that no court has found historic preservation to be a compelling governmental interest).

61. *Cottonwood Christian Ctr.*, 218 F. Supp. at 1228–29.
62. *Westchester Day Sch. II*, 504 F.3d 353.
63. *Id.*
64. 291 F. Supp. 1083, 1094 (C.D. Cal. 2003), *rev'd*, 197 Fed. Appx. 718 (9th Cir. 2006).
65. *Redwood Christian Schs.*, 2007 U.S. Dist. LEXIS 53165, at *10–11.
66. 42 U.S.C. § 2000cc(a)(2).
67. *Westchester Day Sch. II*, 504 F.3d at 353.
68. *See, e.g., id.* at 354 (construction of 44,000-square-foot building, with an estimated cost of $9 million, will affect interstate commerce); *Freedom Baptist Church of Del. County v. Twp. of Middletown*, 204 F. Supp. 2d 857 (E.D. Pa. 2002) (assuming that rental of property and use and development of land implicates interstate commerce prong); *Cottonwood Christian Ctr.*, 218 F. Supp. 2d at 1221 (construction project affects interstate commerce).
69. *DiLaura*, 30 Fed. Appx. at 510 (retreat house); *Cottonwood Christian Ctr.*, 218 F. Supp. 2d at 1221 (church will have televised ministry and bookstore, and will host conferences involving out-of-state participation).
70. *Guru Nanak Sikh Soc'y*, 456 F.3d at 986.
71. *Id.* at 987 (conditional use permit); *see also, e.g., Episcopal Student Found.*, 341 F. Supp. 2d at 699 (demolition permit from a historic commission). *But see Rocky Mountain Christian Church v. Board of County Comm'rs*, 481 F. Supp. 2d 1213, 1223 (D. Colo. 2007) (citing *Grace United Methodist*, 451 F.3d at 653, for the proposition that not every zoning variance scheme constitutes an individualized assessment subject to strict scrutiny under applicable constitutional standards or, hence, under RLUIPA).
72. *Guru Nanak Sikh Soc'y*, 456 F.3d at 987.
73. 366 F.3d at 1229; *see also New Life Ministries v. Charter Twp. of Mt. Morris*, 2006 U.S. Dist. LEXIS 63848, at *9 (E.D. Mich. 2006).

74. 42 U.S.C. § 2000cc(b)(1).
75. 450 F.3d 1295, 1308 (11th Cir. 2006).
76. *Id.* at 1308.
77. *Id.* at 1308–09, citing *Midrash Sephardi*, 366 F.3d at 1230–31.
78. *Midrash Sephardi*, 366 F.3d at 1231.
79. *Id.* at 1220.
80. *Id.* at 1233–35; *see also Vietnamese Buddhism Study Temple v. City of Garden Grove*, 460 F. Supp. 2d 1165, 1175 (C.D. Cal. 2006) (concerns about increased traffic, increased on-street parking, and loss of revenue "simply do not justify facially unequal treatment between a church and a private club" whereby the former is prohibited in an office professional district while the latter is allowed); *New Life Ministries*, 2006 U.S. Dist. LEXIS 63848, at *14–15 (churches are singled out for exclusion from zone where private clubs, civic organizations, theaters, educational institutions, and other assemblies are allowed).
81. *Vision Church*, 468 F.3d at 1004.
82. *Primera Iglesia*, 450 F.3d at 1309, citing *Church of the Lukumi Babalu Aye, Inc. v. City of Hialeah*, 508 U.S. 520 (1993).
83. *Id.* at 1310.
84. *Id.*
85. *Id.* at 1310–11.
86. *Konikov,* 410 F.3d at 1328.
87. *Lighthouse Inst. for Evangelism, Inc. v. City of Long Branch,* 510 F.3d 253, 268 (3d Cir. 2007).
88. *Id.* at 269.
89. *Id.* at 270–72.
90. 42 U.S.C. § 2000cc (b)(2).
91. *Men of Destiny Ministries*, 2006 WL 3219321, at *5.
92. 42 U.S.C. §§ 2000cc(b)(3)(A), (b)(3)(B).
93. *See Redwood Christian Schs. v. County of Alameda,* 2007 U.S. Dist. LEXIS 22626, at *17 (N.D. Cal. 2007) (no basis for exclusion claim where plaintiff already operates a school elsewhere in the county and has been granted several permits for improvements at that site and would be eligible for permits to build at other sites in the county if it chose to move there).
94. *Vision Church*, 468 F.3d at 990 (citing *Sts. Constantine & Helen Greek Orthodox Church*, 396 F.3d at 900 (internal quotations omitted)).

95. *Id.* at 991.
96. *See, e.g., Westchester Day Sch. II*, 504 F.3d at 353–56 (finding RLUIPA not in excess of authority under Commerce Clause or Fourteenth Amendment, and not in violation of Establishment Clause or Tenth Amendment); *Guru Nanak Sikh Soc'y*, 456 F.3d at 992–95 (finding RLUIPA constitutional under the Fourteenth Amendment); *Midrash Sephardi*, 336 F.3d at 1235–43 (upholding RLUIPA against Fourteenth Amendment, Establishment Clause, and Tenth Amendment challenges).
97. 291 F. Supp. 2d 1083, 1097–1102 (C.D. Cal. 2003), *rev'd,* 197 Fed. Appx. 718 (9th Cir. 2006).
98. 291 F. Supp. 2d at 1102–04.
99. 544 U.S. 709 (2005).
100. In a footnote, the Court stated with respect to RLUIPA's land use provisions: "Section 2 of RLUIPA is not at issue here. We therefore express no view on the validity of that part of the Act." *Id.* at 715 n.3.
101. *Murphy v. Zoning Comm'n*, 148 F. Supp. 2d 173 (D. Conn. 2001); *Murphy v. Zoning Comm'n*, 289 F. Supp. 2d 87 (D. Conn. 2003).
102. *Murphy v. New Milford Zoning Comm'n,* 402 F.3d at 347–53 (applying *Williamson County Regional Planning Comm'n v. Hamilton Bank*, 473 U.S. 172 (1985)).
103. 402 F.3d at 352–53; *see also Grace Cmty. Church v. Lenox Twp.*, 544 F.3d 609 (6th Cir. 2008) (upholding dismissal of RLUIPA claim on ripeness grounds where church had made no effort to seek reinstatement of revoked special use permit, or to appeal from or seek reconsideration of revocation decision).
104. *Konikov*, 410 F.3d at 1322.
105. *DiLaura*, 30 Fed. Appx. at 504–05.
106. *Sisters of St. Francis Health Servs., Inc. v. Morgan County*, 397 F. Supp. 2d 1032, 1048 (D. Ind. 2005).
107. 42 U.S.C. § 2000cc-3(e); *see C.L.U.B.*, 342 F.3d at 759 (by amending its zoning, the city avoided RLUIPA's preemptive effect).
108. *League of Residential Neighborhood Advocates v. City of Los Angeles*, 498 F.3d 1052 (9th Cir. 2007).

How Local Government Can Nip RLUIPA Claims in the Bud

7

Dwight H. Merriam, FAICP

This chapter is written from the perspective of a local government lawyer (and occasional planner). It offers advice about how municipalities can protect themselves from RLUIPA claims and liability. The focus is on avoiding claims in the first instance and then, if litigation ensues, ways in which government can defend itself. RLUIPA presents a dual threat to a municipality: first, the potential for financial liability in the form of money damages and attorneys' fees paid to a prevailing religious claimant or paid to settle a claim, and second, the prospect of litigation supplanting local decision making processes whereby a court substitutes its judgment for that of local officials.[1]

Know Where You Are So You Know Where You're Going

Assuming you started at the beginning of this book and have read straight through to this point, you should have a good sense of all the basic elements of a RLUIPA claim. If you would not be comfortable giving a three-minute discourse on what could be considered "religious exercise" and another three-minute speech on the factors a court will weigh in determining whether government has imposed a "substantial burden," you may wish to restudy those sections. They are essential to avoiding liability.

At the same time, it must be conceded that no one will feel truly comfortable answering these two critical issues because neither Congress nor the courts have defined the boundaries of either religious exercise or substantial burden. The law of RLUIPA is organic, building on incremental precedent from diverse factual and cultural settings and creating an often murky admixture of holdings, dictum, and musings. Lawyers are often asked: "What's the chance we will win?" When it comes to RLUIPA claims, the response is almost certain to contain more "ifs" per line than most opinions.

The challenge is to put that admittedly limited knowledge to work to help you—as a governmental planner, lawyer, administrator or public official—to eliminate or minimize the potential for governmental liability. The stakes are high. A court could direct the government to approve an application contrary to the community's plan and regulations; there is the potential for money damages (although this remains uncertain); and attorneys' fees can be awarded even if the matter is resolved short of trial.

> **Practice Pointer:** Don't settle these cases in any way, including granting a partial approval under the threat of RLUIPA, without full mutual releases from all liability including attorneys' fees.

The first reaction might be to call in the lawyers, but that could be counterproductive. As the psychologist Abraham Maslow (1908–1970) said: "When the only tool you have is a hammer, then every problem begins to look like a nail." Get a few lawyers in a room and throw them a hunk of raw RLUIPA, and they'll gnaw at it like, well, what they are, lawyers: burden of proof, elements of the claim, discovery, depositions, venue, subpoenas, and suddenly your head is spinning.

Listen to your mothers who, like mine, said: "An ounce of prevention is worth a pound of cure," and "A stitch in time saves nine." Back up a few steps in the process and start working on your RLUIPA defense before any religious organization even thinks about wielding that sword. It's almost always too late when the lawyers come aboard for damage control and extrication expeditions.

Plan, and Then Plan Some More

Another aphorism: the best defense is a good offense. Plan for religious uses. You plan for schools and gas stations; plan for religious uses. Conduct surveys. Know what their needs are. Your community might grow 10 percent in population over the next ten years. Presently, the religious assembly needs are being met with one thousand seats. In ten years you may need at least one hundred more seats, perhaps in different locations. Church-run schools have shown dramatic increases in enrollments. Will that trend continue? What do religious leaders foresee as their needs? Will local campuses suffice, or do they aspire to larger facilities? Are there forms of communication, such as Web-based services, which could reduce the need for public assembly space or change the peak times of use? Are they planning multiple services, or services on more days, in order to handle any increases in membership and attendance? Are they branching out into other areas, such as providing primary and secondary education, senior day care, after-school recreational programs, meals on wheels, affordable housing, and alcohol and drug rehabilitation? The list of potentially relevant planning considerations goes on and on. Don't wait for these activities to land within the reach of RLUIPA. Treat them as a planning issue.

> **Practice Pointer:** Generally, treat religious land use activities as you would similar secular activities, such as other places of public assembly. Never restrict religious activities more than you would restrict nonreligious activities of the same type.

Of course it would be unwise to give preference to religious uses because of the potential for being skewered by that other provision in the First Amendment—the establishment clause—which prohibits government from promoting religion or favoring one religion over another. But you must account for them in your planning as you would any secular use with similar characteristics, such as schools, places of public assembly, and offices.

The other side of planning is the allocation of present and future use demands to the exclusion of other uses. Is there a need to protect agricultural production to lower the community's carbon footprint and preserve capacity for future generations? If so, that land cannot become a parking lot, whether for a church or another nonagricultural use. Is there a need for a pedestrian friendly community, especially for the retiring boomers, and the increased, mutually supportive human and economic activity that comes from more feet on the street? If so, is there a plan for concentrating places of public assembly—secular as well as religious—in central areas?

Practice Pointer: Keep chanting the mantra: "I will plan for all future land uses comprehensively."

No court has yet held that aesthetics alone, even historic preservation, is a compelling government interest sufficient to fend off a RLUIPA claim once a substantial burden has been shown. But compelling governmental objectives may be found in measures to protect the public's health and safety. There is a chance that a court might find, under the right circumstances, a compelling interest in protecting a community's sole source aquifer from pollution by a megachurch parking lot or preventing traffic hazards.[2]

Put the heavyweight governmental objectives out front.[3] Identify where risks to the public's health and safety might exist. Don't bother with lightweight objectives, important as they may be to you as planner, like "scenic vistas"—they may just end up diluting the objectives that might be compelling. This is what happened in the famous *Lucas* case in 1992.[4] The state of South Carolina restricted building on beachfronts that were especially likely to experience erosion because people could be killed and property destroyed, but the state also mentioned it was good for tourism to save these areas. The courts took note of the latter "lightweight" objective and, to some extent, lost sight of the life safety issue.

Audit Your Own Regulations as if You Were Suing Yourself

Step back from your own regulations and look at them as an outsider. If you are psychologically or politically unable to do that, then hire someone to do it for you. The objective is to drill deep into your present regulatory structure to find any underlying weaknesses that could become the basis for liability.

Ask yourself this critical question: Is there anything in your code that allows a school, day care center, or place of public assembly where you would not allow a religious land use or analogous use operated by a religious institution? If the answer is yes, you should probably eliminate the disparity by expanding the rights of religious institutions to equal those of nonsectarian organizations.

Based on your planning studies, do you have sufficient land in your community for the expansion of clearly religious activities such as worship and religious education, as well as for other activities commonly conducted by religious organizations that arguably might be claimed as part of a religious use (such as athletic facilities for church-sponsored leagues and functions on church campuses)? Remember that the market is imperfect, and many potentially developable sites may not be for sale. You might want to err on the side of zoning to provide an excess of potential sites for such uses, so that you will be better able to defend against the argument that your community has taken advantage of a constrained market to exclude new religious activities and related facilities.

Are you using the special use permit or conditional use—both of them in most jurisdictions are administrative and discretionary—for religious uses? If the answer is yes, allegations could be made that the process itself imposes an undue and substantial burden on the religious applicant, or that the discretion has been exercised in a way that disfavors religion or discriminates among denominations. It is generally better, from a RLUIPA strategy standpoint, to treat religious uses through neutral and generally applicable zoning laws than to do so through site-specific discretionary approvals.

RLUIPA is a statute of limited jurisdiction, and when a government undertakes an "individualized assessment" of a proposed religious use of a property under its land use regulations, it pulls one of the triggers for the substantial burden inquiry. Arguably, a special use permit or similar type of administrative review would be such an "individualized assessment." But a law of general applicability, for example, that sets performance standards for all assembly uses would not be. In many jurisdictions it may be possible to convert the conditional use or special permit process into nondiscretionary performance standards.[5] The as-of-right use with strict standards, including traffic impacts and density limits by floor area ratio and lot coverage, can provide just about all you need without having to make a site-specific decision as to a particular use.

Practice Pointer: Classify religious uses either as permitted as of right or not permitted at all in particular districts, if you can do so without compromising your comprehensive plan for growth and development.

If you decide to rezone properties to eliminate or restrict religious uses from certain areas, be sensitive to the reality that if a religious organization owns the site it might have vested rights in the former zoning, and if you rezone property while a religious organization is considering purchasing it (or shortly after it has purchased it), the rezoning may appear to be reactionary or retaliatory.[6] It might be more prudent to err on the side of expanding vested rights, rather than eliminating or limiting those rights.

Practice Pointer: A last resort, and one that should be avoided, is a moratorium on religious uses. Moratoria have not fared well except when there is an overarching public health and safety need, when it is applicable to all or most development, and when it is intended to be a very short "planning pause" such as six months.

Prepare the Front Desk

Planners and land use administrators often cause more damage than they realize by innocently answering what seems to be a straightforward question and, in doing so, inadvertently create unwarranted expectations. Many times such questions are not what they seem. No one at the front desk can ever really know who is speaking for whom, and what may be intended. For example, a religious group may contract secretly to purchase property for a new facility. The group may have its representative inquire of the planning and building department what is and is not permitted on the property without revealing its plans. A problem may be ahead for the municipality if the answer is incorrect, or even if it is accurate but suggests, for example, that among the range of apparently allowed uses, there is great local enthusiasm for taxpaying business uses and dislike of tax-exempt institutions.

If the inquiry is other than a run-of-the-mill question concerning an as-of-right use such as a single-family home, it may be best simply to offer a copy of the code and suggest that the individual consult with others. It might even be useful to give every person who makes any type of inquiry a one-page statement of the resources that are available through the municipal offices. In the process of providing that document, the public's accessibility to the information is increased, and there is an opportunity to give an express warning that most land use approvals involve federal, state, and local complexities and interpretations requiring professional assistance. It can also be mentioned that anyone undertaking a land development project should seek the advice of design and development professionals and legal counsel as needed.

The other side of this coin is that it is important for public servants to serve the public and it is also important that a municipality demonstrate its willingness to assist religious organizations in meeting the terms of the regulations and moving their projects through the approval process in an efficient and orderly manner. The best way to balance the need to protect casual conversations from leading to untenable expectations while still providing a high level of service is to bring the potential applicants in front of local boards and commissions as soon as possible. It is much easier to manage communications when senior staff and experienced chairpersons are present. Consider a pre-application process with a public meeting, where potential applicants can explain to the public officials their anticipated requests. The objective is not to preempt, but to have some broader input and preserve record evidence that the potential applicant was helped in every way possible and was given the best advice by the appropriate authorities even before coming in with the application.

The pre-application meeting may be counterintuitive. Can it really help to start discussing a development project before it comes in as a formal application? In many, if not most, cases the answer is yes. Applicants often become economically and psychologically committed to detailed plans when they spend substantial money on them before getting any real feedback from decision makers. The pre-application meeting in the early stage provides a forum for give-and-take that can avert serious mistakes. Imagine a commissioner observing at such a meeting: "I see by your sketch plan that you have your major entrance on Elm Street. There is a draft amendment to the town's Master Plan addressing the serious traffic congestion we have on that street from the recent development of the Mega Mart. If you reoriented the site plan to use Oak Street exclusively, I think it will avoid some serious problems for you." Helpful observations such as this might circumvent a denial or conditional approval requiring a costly and extensive redesign.

Win by Avoiding the Simple Mistakes

I confess to being a poor tennis player. When forced to play, I have a simple strategy—just get the ball back over the net. Nothing fancy, no slamming or spinning, no driving the opponent to the very back corner . . . just get it over the net.

Most of the difficulty I encounter in defending RLUIPA claims arises out of a careless, thoughtless, uninformed, casual, or glib passing remark, or even a nervous attempt at humor in a highly charged situation. No, these "one off" remarks usually don't create liability, but neutralizing them from a hearing or deposition transcript can be Sisyphean.

Some would call what needs to be done "coaching," a pejorative term. This is better described as sensitizing and helping people understand the limits of their authority under RLUIPA.

In one case in which the municipality was ultimately held liable under RLUIPA, the decision makers rejected the reasonable advice of their planners—twice.[7] It is not that elected officials have to do what their planners tell them, but when the expert advice is sought—twice—and rejected with no apparent overriding public policy considerations, it is reasonable and appropriate for a court to look at that process with more scrutiny.

Practice Pointer: You get what you ask for. When seeking professional advice, be careful in telling your consultant what you want reviewed. If it is only about traffic, say so.

In a recent instance regarding a synagogue proposal, which so far has not ripened into a RLUIPA suit, a member of a local historic preservation board commented that she didn't think it was a problem having the synagogue in the historic district but that the proposed Star of David on the top might not be appropriate. It is hard to imagine how the principal symbol of the Jewish faith could be excluded entirely. This type of comment at the very first pre-application meeting demonstrated a lack of knowledge about the law and a high degree of insensitivity about the applicant's religion. It was widely reported, and set the wrong tone for the commencement of the proceeding. Had this commission been briefed in advance on the essentials of RLUIPA and the importance of maintaining an appropriate public record, this rocky start could have been avoided.

Practice Pointer: If a public official makes a mistake, for example by saying something plainly wrong during a public proceeding or in a written statement, the best thing to do in most cases is to admit wrongdoing and apologize as part of an attempt to cleanse the record.

Practice Makes Perfect

A board or commission with land use decision making authority should be put through its paces to educate the members about

RLUIPA compliance. Prepare a hypothetical application and conduct a mock hearing. Stir the pot. Egg them on; taunt them a little, from all sides. Don't forget a gaggle of angry neighbors. Nothing pushes the buttons of public officials more than getting caught in crossfire.

Test their anger management. See if they know how far RLUIPA reaches. Ask, for example, for a bowling alley for a religious group to provide recreational opportunities for its members. Take that up a notch by saying that it will be a refuge for troubled teenagers. See if the officials ask for information on the religious group's mission. During the later critique, ellicit a discussion about whether a bowling alley is an integral part of the religious expression, and then challenge the officials to think about whether they were tougher on the religious group than they might have been on a for-profit bowling alley or a nonreligious charitable group that used bowling as therapy. The military uses extensive post-exercise briefings to provide constructive criticism. It is much better to ferret out problems when the stakes are no more than a little rush of embarrassment.

Another approach, one that we use in procedural due process training, is to completely script a religious use hearing, and have public officials, staff, and other volunteers read the parts. Build as many problems and errors into the script as you can. The obvious ones will bring laughter. The subtle ones can stimulate discussion during the post-exercise critique.

Make the Record

Nothing is more important in successfully defending against a RLUIPA claim than a complete, comprehensive, and compelling record of rational decision making based on the pursuit of legitimate governmental objectives. Once the RLUIPA claimant gets past the "substantial burden" hurdle, the government must assert and prove "compelling" interests for its action. One example of how *not* to do it is provided by the case of *Guru Nanak Sikh Society of Yuba City v. County of Sutter,* a Ninth Circuit decision from 2006.[8] In the end, the Ninth Circuit held that the county had imposed a substantial burden on Guru Nanak because the stated reasons and history behind the denial at issue, and the fact that there had been a previous denial of Guru Nanak's application to build a temple on a parcel of land zoned "residential," "lessened to a significantly great extent the possibility of Guru Nanak constructing a temple in the future."[9] Moreover, the court said the county did not assert, nor prove, that there was any compelling interest for its denial of the proposal for the temple. The real story lies in the details of the process, and the failure to create a supportive record.

Guru Nanak first applied for a conditional use permit for a temple on 1.89 acres. The county planning division recommended approval of the application subject to conditions consistent with the general plan, but the planning commission voted unanimously to deny the permit. "The denial was based on fears voiced by residents that the resulting noise and traffic would interfere with the existing neighborhood."[10] In response to the denial, and mindful of the concerns expressed about the perceived conflicts between the temple use and a residential neighborhood, Guru Nanak went looking for another site. It found 28.79 acres in an agricultural district, and proposed converting an existing 2,300-square-foot single-family residence and increasing the size of the building by about five hundred square feet to a temple of about 2,850 square feet. This building was intended to serve no more than seventy-five members and was to be used as a place of religious celebration, an assembly hall, and for weddings. It applied for a conditional use permit for this purpose. Churches are allowed nowhere in the county as of right. Nonetheless, various boards and agencies ultimately approved the proposal subject to numerous conditions, and the planning division issued a "mitigated negative declaration," which, freely translated, means that the proposed temple would not create a significant environmental impact because the mitigation measures would reduce any impacts to insignificant levels.

After a public hearing, the planning commission approved the application by a vote of four to three. The four-member board of supervisors held a hearing on appeals brought by several neighbors, reversed the planning commission's approval, and denied Guru Nanak's application. The supervisors gave various reasons for the reversal, including that the property was agricultural and should remain so, that it was "too far away from the city" and would not promote orderly growth, that the use would be detrimental to surrounding agricultural uses, and that Guru Nanak should locate a church closer to other existing churches. Two of the commissioners characterized the proposal as "leapfrog development" given its location away from existing infrastructure.

In a lengthy decision, the Ninth Circuit analyzed the decision making process in detail and found it lacking. The court affirmed the trial court's order granting summary judgment for Guru Nanak, and enjoined the county to immediately approve the conditional use permit application. Because the interpretation and application of the county's regulations in denying the application a second time was found to have imposed a substantial burden on Guru Nanak, the county was obligated to prove, which it did not, that there were "narrowly tailored, compelling reasons" to deny the application.

> **Practice Pointer:** First, eliminate any legitimate basis for claiming that a site-specific review and denial will create a substantial burden by clearly identifying other alternatives including, as appropriate, scaled-back or redesigned development on the same site, or development on other more suitable sites in specified areas. Second, if there is concern the court will find the denial or conditional approval to be a substantial burden, then make sure the record is replete with evidence detailing which safety or other compelling governmental interests were furthered by the denial or conditional approval, and why that outcome was the least restrictive means of addressing those interests.

Don't imagine that government will lose simply because it denied a conditional use permit. The Supreme Court of Oregon, in *Presiding Bishop of the Church of Jesus Christ of Latter-Day Saints v. City of West Linn,*[11] held that the denial of a conditional use permit to build a new meeting house did not constitute a "substantial burden" even though the denial had "several adverse consequences for the church's effort to build a meeting house."[12] The city had directed the church to submit a new permit application to use a greater portion of the available lot, to provide additional buffering, and to submit required noise studies. This process imposed additional expenses on the church but was not a "substantial burden" because it appeared the conditions could be met and "nothing in the record indicated that the city would not approve a revised application."

If *Guru Nanak* is the violet of the visible spectrum, the 2008 decision of the Connecticut Supreme Court in *Cambodian Buddhist Society of Connecticut, Inc. v. Planning and Zoning Commission of the Town of Newtown* is at the far end, hundreds of nanometers away.[13]

In 1999 the society purchased a ten-acre tract with two acres of wetlands and a five-acre pond, and a home in which four Buddhist monks took up residence. The site was in a farming and residential zone where religious institutions are allowed by special exception. The local land use agency denied an application for approval of a 7,618-square-foot building (1,618-square-foot meditation temple and 6,000-square-foot meeting hall) with 148 parking spaces to accommodate 450 society members. Its reasons for denial included that it would be inconsistent with a "quiet single-family residential neighborhood with a rural setting," health treatment uses rumored to be conducted on site were not permitted, the existing volume of traffic would double or triple, the temple design was not in harmony with the neighborhood, and the water and septic system did not meet regulations.

The Connecticut Supreme Court held that RLUIPA didn't apply. The court reached that determination by first holding that "the substantial burden provision of RLUIPA does not apply to neutral and generally applicable land use regulations that are intended to protect the public health and safety, such as those at issue in the present case."[14]

After a long march through First Amendment jurisprudence and its relationship to interpreting "substantial burden" in RLUIPA, the court settled on case law determinations as to "when the substantial burden provision applies to government conduct in the first instance." That, in turn, forced the court to analyze what an "individualized assessment" might be because RLUIPA, by its express terms, limits applicability of the substantial burden provision to those instances where there are individualized assessments.

In a precedent-setting act of prestidigitation that won the day for Newtown, the court concluded that while Newtown's regulations gave the agency some discretion, they did not permit the agency to apply them to religious facilities differently than they were applied to other special exception uses such as clubs, hospitals, landfills, and private schools. Therefore, the special exception regulations did not allow for an "individualized assessment" and, consequentially the substantial burden analysis was never reached. Importantly, the land use agency had the discretion in the regulations to apply them in a discriminatory manner, but it did not. It was not the regulations *per se* or the procedural nature of the discretionary special exception authority, but the decision made by the agency ("motivated not by religious bigotry but by neutral considerations") that defined whether it was an individualized assessment. Court watchers and RLUIPA aficionados will be standing by to see if other courts follow this line of reasoning. Until then, local governments will be citing this decision every chance they get.

Preserve the Evidence

The hot button issues in complex RLUIPA civil litigation cases are spoliation and electronic discovery (e-discovery). "Spoliation" looks like a typographic error, doesn't it? Spoliation is derived from an Anglo-French word of the fifteenth century meaning to plunder. In the wild and wonderful world of discovery it means the willful destruction of evidence that otherwise should be preserved and potentially available to a litigation opponent. The short version of the big problem is that if any documentation (letter, report, meeting note, phone record, and even e-mail and other electronic documentation) is prepared or received in the normal course of business, or is potential evidence relative to an issue that it is reasonably probable would be subject to litigation, then whoever has that evidence should not destroy it.

Practice Pointer: If you do not already have a records-retention policy consistent with federal and state law that permits you to destroy documents and requires you to preserve others for express periods of time, you should develop one to make sure that everyone knows the rules and follows them.

The newly amended Federal Rules of Civil Procedure expressly refer to the discovery of "electronically stored information," commonly referred to as ESI in "electronic discovery."[15] Electronically stored information includes "writings, drawings, graphs, charts, photographs, sound recordings, images, and other data or data compilations stored in any medium from which information can be obtained, . . ." and parties in federal litigation may "inspect, copy, test, or sample any designated documents or electronically stored information . . . ." The sheer volume of electronically stored information, not to mention the sometimes damaging content found within, has created an almost incalculable burden on litigants. The cost of organizing and producing electronically stored information in a single case can be several million dollars. A formal records-retention policy and organized electronic document storage and retrieval system can protect government from unnecessary liability.

Practice Pointer: Start with two simple steps. First, put all of your local government computer systems on a single server with adequate backup so that records can be more easily retrieved. Second, establish governmental e-mail accounts for all elected and appointed officials and staff, and prohibit anyone from using their personal e-mail accounts for any government-related communications. This latter step will avoid the need to potentially produce personal computers and data files in the discovery process.

In the End . . .

In the end, what you do at the beginning can make the difference between success and failure. Good planning (taking into account forecasting space needs, religion-neutral regulations, and adequately trained staff and decision makers), decisions based on substantial evidence, and proper records management can eliminate a large part of the potential liability for local governments. Our doctors tell us to eat right and exercise, but we still have nearly 25,000 cardiologists in the country.[16] It is similarly unlikely that the RLUIPA defense bar will soon disappear.

Notes

1. I draw on many sources in this chapter and cite them specifically where it is appropriate. Otherwise, the text reflects the case law and literature generally. I want to expressly acknowledge that I draw extensively on two useful sources that apparently are not generally in the public domain, but which I can make available to the reader if they send me an electronic mail message to dmerriam@rc.com. The first of these articles is by Jeffrey T. Melching of Rutan & Tucker LLP and was presented to the City Attorneys Association of Los Angeles County at its spring 2003 retreat. That paper is entitled, "The Religious Land Use and Institutionalized Persons Act of 2000 (RLUIPA): What's a City to Do When a Church Comes to Town?" The second is a recent short presentation by a lawyer who has labored in the RLUIPA trenches, most recently in an important case against a municipality, *Westchester Day Sch. v. Vill. of the Mamaroneck*, 504 F.3d 338 (2d Cir. 2007). That paper is by Kevin J. Plunkett of DelBello Donnellan Weingarten Wise & Wiederkehr, LLP, and was presented to the New York State Bar Association Municipal Law Section's annual meeting on October 20, 2007. It is entitled, "Religious Land Use and Institutionalized Persons Act (RLUIPA): Dos and Don'ts for Municipal Attorneys When Advising Municipal Board Members, Staff and Consultants."
2. *See Mont. Envtl. Info. Ctr. v. MDEC*, 296 Mont. 207 (1999).
3. *See Westchester Day Sch. v. Vill. of the Mamaroneck*, 280 F. Supp. 2d 242, 230 (S.D.N.Y. 2003) ("traffic concerns have never been deemed compelling government interests"); *Murphy v. New Milford Zoning Comm'n*, 402 F.3d 342 (2d Cir. 2005); *Trinity Assembly of God of Baltimore City, Inc. v. People's Counsel for Baltimore County*, 2008 WL 314717 (Md. App. 2008).
4. *Lucas v. S.C. Coastal Council*, 505 U.S. 1003 (1992).
5. For a case on point discussing the ins and outs of conditional use permits as compared with the alternative of the legislative planned unit development in a safe haven of the as-of-right approach, see *Sts. Constantine & Helen Greek Orthodox Church, Inc. v. City of New Berlin*, 396 F.3d 895 (7th Cir. 2005).

6. *See Petra Presbyterian Church v. Vill. of Northbrook*, 489 F.3d 846 (7th Cir. 2007); *see also Cypress Christian Ctr. v. Cypress Redevelopment Agency*, 218 F. Supp. 2d 1203 (C.D. Cal. 2002).
7. *Guru Nanak Sikh Soc'y of Yuba City v. County of Sutter,* 456 F.3d 978 (9th Cir. 2006).
8. *Id.*
9. *Id.* at 981.
10. *Id.* at 982.
11. 338 Or. 453, 111 P.3d 1123 (2005).
12. 338 Or. at 467, 111 P.3d at 1130. "For the purposes of this opinion, we assume without deciding that the city's denial of the CUP constituted an individualized assessment as that term is used in 42 USC § 2000cc(a)(2)(C)." 338 Or. at 463 n.5, 111 P.3d at 1128 n.5.
13. 285 Conn. 381 (2008).
14. *Id.* at 400.
15. Fed. R. Civ. P. 34(a).
16. W. Bruce Frye, *Cardiology Workforce: A Shortage, Not a Surplus*, Health Affairs, Feb. 4, 2004, *available at* http://content.healthaffairs.org/cgi/reprint/hlthaff.w4.64v1; Locumtens.com, Cardiology Career and Resource Center, http://www.locumtenens.com/cardiology-careers/main.aspx (last visited Mar. 17, 2009).

8

RLUIPA Challenges: An Ounce of Prevention Is Worth a Pound of Cure

Alan Weinstein

Advising local officials on how to avoid a RLUIPA claim is no easy task. After moving beyond the obvious things like "don't totally exclude churches" or "don't regulate churches in a discriminatory manner" (for example, requiring churches to obtain a conditional use approval while similar secular uses are allowed "as of right")—it is difficult to prescribe a list of *specific* dos and don'ts. Each potential RLUIPA claim arises within the context of a particular site and the implementation of a specific land use code. Thus, when it comes to RLUIPA, the adage that "the devil is in the details" is particularly apt: it is difficult to provide specific guidance absent knowledge of those details. Further, similar "RLUIPA facts" can yield very different outcomes depending on the attitudes and knowledge of the parties involved.

Local government reactions to potential RLUIPA claims have run the gamut from immediate unconditional surrender at a church's mere mention of RLUIPA, to good-faith efforts at compromise, to willingness—perhaps even eagerness—to litigate the case all the way to the U.S. Supreme Court. These differing reactions are partially explained by the facts of particular RLUIPA disputes, but another critical factor is the attitude of the parties. If either or both of the parties is unwilling to acknowledge, or minimizes, the legitimacy of the other's concerns, conflict rather than compromise is the more likely outcome. Thus, for example, some religious leaders may believe that RLUIPA affords them almost *carte blanche* when it comes to complying with land use regulations. Similarly, some local officials may lack sensitivity to the legitimate needs of a particular religious group or, on rare occasion, actually view a particular religion or sect in a negative light.

A final factor making specific advice difficult is that the courts have not provided clear-cut guidance in the RLUIPA decisions issued to date. This may be due, in part, to the unique circumstances of each case, and also to the fact that courts have different interpretations of RLUIPA's provisions.

Proactive Steps Local Governments Might Take to Avoid a RLUIPA Claim

When it comes to facing an *actual* RLUIPA claim, local government officials need to understand that some claims should *not* be avoided. RLUIPA was enacted to address congressional concerns about unfair treatment of religious land uses, not to provide religious land uses with immunity from land use regulation.[1] Local officials need to give serious consideration to any claim that a land use regulation violates RLUIPA but, if after such consideration they decide that the claim lacks merit, they should not accede to a violation of a legitimate land use regulation merely to avoid possible litigation.[2]

Local officials can seek to avoid a potential RLUIPA claim both proactively and reactively. Proactively, local governments should examine land use regulations affecting religious uses, and how those regulations have been applied. At a minimum, zoning ordinances should provide reasonable locations for new, or expanding, houses of worship and accessory religious uses such as schools.

While providing such options might not be particularly difficult in newer, less-developed communities, it can be a problem in older communities that are almost fully developed. Such communities might find that their current zoning effectively precludes houses of worship from residential areas because no sites are available, and severely restricts their location in business and industrial areas, either because religious uses are seen as incompatible in such zones or out of a desire to maintain the city's tax base. Where locational options are effectively nonexistent or extremely limited, a local government should undertake a planning study that seeks to determine how it can accommodate the needs of religious uses without unduly harming surrounding property owners.

Local governments should also examine whether they are making adequate options for "social service" uses such as shelters for the homeless or victims of domestic abuse and facilities to feed the homeless and indigent. The claims of religious institutions that a local government must allow them to "minister to the poor" at a location of their choosing is blunted when a zoning code designates reasonable sites for both secular and religious groups to provide such services.

Historic preservation ordinances should also be reviewed. As a rule, such ordinances should not allow landmark designation of the interior of a sanctuary without consent of the religious institution,[3] and should contain a "hardship" exemption that could be applied to a designated structure if the church meets appropriate criteria.[4]

Local governments should review the procedural requirements of their land use regulations to ensure that they are administered fairly and in a nondiscriminatory manner as applied to religious institutions. Officials need to make sure that land use procedures do not overtly or inadvertently grant religious uses favorable or unfavorable treatment in the land use regulatory process, and should ensure that applications from religious uses are treated no differently than similar applications from secular uses.

Finally, local elected officials should consider arranging for "sensitivity training" for themselves and other public employees to enhance their awareness of religious differences and the need to provide equal treatment to all religious adherents and institutions. It is far less costly to conduct such training before a lack of "sensitivity" to religious differences results in a RLUIPA claim than to do so afterwards while simultaneously defending the claim.[5]

Reactive Steps Local Governments Should Take to Avoid a RLUIPA Claim

While providing specific substantive guidance on avoiding a potential claim is difficult, guidance on procedural matters is more straightforward. Local government officials and staff need to be aware that when dealing with an enforcement action or an application for a land use approval by a church, extra care is advisable, just as it is with other land uses—such as adult entertainment businesses, wireless communications towers, or signs and billboards—that have legal protection beyond the norm.

For example, when government employees and officials meet with principals or representatives of a church to discuss a land use application, they would be well advised to conclude the meeting by confirming with church officials—in writing—the precise points of agreement or disagreement in that discussion and then follow up with a letter or e-mail reiterating that understanding, and requesting notification if there is any disagreement. This practice can help to avoid "we said/they said" disputes that sometimes lead to litigation.[6]

When enforcement actions target a religious use, an internal review process can provide an additional layer of care. The goal is not to exempt churches from enforcement of land use regulations, but rather to ensure that neither churches generally, nor any particular church, are being singled out for more frequent or severe enforcement that could form the basis for a discriminatory treatment claim under RLUIPA.

Cities should also be extremely cautious about departing from well-established precedents when handling a church's land use application. Such a departure can easily lead to a potential RLUIPA claim. For example, in *Hollywood Community Synagogue, Inc. v. City of Hollywood, Florida* (2006),[7] the plaintiff synagogue applied for a conditional use permit that would allow it to use two houses on the edge of a residential district for religious worship and study. The city granted the permit, but for a term of only one year, after which the application would have to be reconsidered. The city had reviewed many such applications in the past from both churches and secular uses, and had never previously granted only a "temporary" permit. This different treatment of the plaintiff's application ultimately formed one aspect of a successful RLUIPA claim that led to a settlement in which the city paid the plaintiff two million dollars in damages.[8] In another case, the district court ruled that the city's refusal to even accept a church's zoning permit application—surely a departure from normal procedures—constituted a substantial burden on religion.[9]

The big question for local governments, of course, is how they should respond when a church makes a land use application or challenges an enforcement action. The starting point to evaluate whether a potential RLUIPA claim can (or should) be avoided is to determine whether RLUIPA is a valid factor: Does the potential claim fall within the protection of the statute? Remember that RLUIPA applies only to "land use regulations," that is, zoning and historic preservation. Thus, while some churches have brought a RLUIPA challenge to an exercise of eminent domain, except for dicta in a footnote in one case, every court that has considered the issue has ruled that an exercise of eminent domain is *not* a land use regulation and thus not governed by RLUIPA.[10]

Other cases have found no jurisdictional basis for a RLUIPA claim where: a city annexed land owned by a church,[11] a city decided to develop a previously dedicated roadway located between two church-owned lots,[12] a city decided to demolish an old church rather than transfer it to a clergyman,[13] and a city denied a telecommunications company a permit to construct a cell tower on a golf course and a neighboring synagogue sought to invoke RLUIPA jurisdiction as a basis for intervening in the applicant's challenge to the denial.[14] Other types of regulatory actions that are clearly outside RLUIPA's jurisdiction include: building or fire safety permits, utility connection permits, and other types of "public health and safety" permits that are outside of either zoning or historical preservation codes.

If a permit application or enforcement action is within the subject matter jurisdiction of RLUIPA, the next step in determining whether there could be a valid claim is to determine whether it falls within one of RLUIPA's three jurisdictional elements: individualized assessments, affecting interstate commerce, or involving federal funding. These jurisdictional elements are found only in the "substantial burden" section of RLUIPA, and thus would not have to be satisfied if an enforcement action or denial of a permit application could be challenged as violating the "equal terms," "nondiscrimination," or "exclusions and limits" sections of RLUIPA.[15] Where a potential claimant could assert that the regulation or its implementation places a "substantial burden" on religious exercise, the claimant must further show that one of these jurisdictional elements has been met.

Most "substantial burden" claims under RLUIPA have relied on the "individualized assessments" element, which can easily be met when the church is applying for a conditional use permit, variance, or another form of approval where there is opportunity for the exercise of discretion.[16] In contrast, although granting or denying a zoning change is clearly discretionary, and thus would seem to be an "individualized assessment,"[17] one court has ruled that it is not, presumably because it viewed the rezoning as a legislative act involving broad policy and political judgments.[18] Courts have also proven to be relatively sympathetic to the claim that a substantial burden on religious exercise successfully invokes the "affects interstate commerce" jurisdictional element.[19] In short, meeting the jurisdictional element should not pose a significant problem for a church as it considers a potential substantial burden RLUIPA claim.

We now come to the crux of the matter: on a substantive basis, what should local governments do—or refrain from doing—to avoid a potential RLUIPA claim when considering a permit application or an enforcement action? In very general terms, local governments have tended to prevail against RLUIPA challenges when they can demonstrate that the restrictions placed on a church: (1) do not target religious uses for discriminatory treatment, (2) are necessary to achieve valid land use regulatory goals, and (3) do not force the church to cease religious worship. Conversely, churches have tended to prevail when local government was unable to meet these same criteria.

Guidance becomes more difficult when we move away from generalities. "Substantial burden" claims are particularly difficult in this regard. RLUIPA does not define "substantial burden." The drafters' intent was that courts would define the term in line with prior precedent. That precedent strongly suggests that courts would be extremely unlikely to find a land use regulation had imposed a substantial burden on a church, but that has not proven to be so. While the majority of substantial burden claims have failed, courts have found in a number of cases that land use regulations indeed imposed a substantial burden on the exercise of religion.[20] These differing outcomes can be explained, in part, by the different ways that courts have articulated what constitutes a "substantial burden." For example, the Seventh Circuit has interpreted "substantial burden" both quite narrowly: a substantial burden is imposed only when regulations make religious exercise "impracticable" within the jurisdiction generally,[21] and more broadly: a substantial burden can be found based on delay, uncertainty, and expense.[22]

These interpretations, when combined with the unique factual settings of each case, have yielded outcomes that are difficult to reconcile. For example, the Eleventh Circuit found no substantial burden when a synagogue was prohibited from locating in a downtown business district,[23] while the Ninth Circuit upheld a district court ruling that found a substantial burden where the city had denied approval for a church's preferred site in a downtown business district.[24]

Avoiding a RLUIPA claim based on the other provisions of the statute might be easier. Local officials obviously need to steer clear of even the appearance of unequal treatment or discrimination—whether for or against—a particular church or sect, and should treat religious uses the same as secular uses. But even here, some court decisions suggest guidance is not so easy. For example, in the Eleventh Circuit case noted above, religious uses were not allowed in the central business district where secular assembly uses were allowed, but churches could locate in residential districts where secular assembly uses were prohibited.[25] From either a planning or legal perspective, one might argue that while the treatment of the secular and religious uses was *different*, it did not violate RLUIPA's equal terms provision because the code "equalized" its treatment of the uses.

The best advice to local officials on avoidance of potential RLUIPA claims may well be less legal and more common sense: treat church representatives fairly and with respect, and try to engage in a good-faith effort to craft a reasonable compromise between the church's request and the city's land use policies. As a federal judge noted in one of the first reported RLUIPA cases, which involved a city's enforcement action to limit the number of attendees at prayer services held in a private home:

> Even absent a federal statute, one would expect that, before banning an ongoing private religious gathering, public officials in a free and tolerant society would enter into a dialogue with the participants to determine if the legitimate safety concerns of the neighbors could be voluntarily allayed. Particularly where the participants are enjoined by religious teachings to "do unto others" as they would have done unto them, it is not unreasonable to expect the parties to be able to agree on means of reducing the impact of weekly prayer meetings on this small cul-de-sac without undermining the benefit that participants seek to derive from the practice of their faith.[26]

The judge enjoined both sides to enter into dialogue to seek a reasonable compromise. Avoiding a potential claim is not solely within the discretion of local officials. Church officials have, in some cases, been dismissive of legitimate land use concerns and pursued claims that bordered on the frivolous, but where both sides are willing to seek common ground, there is often room for compromise.

Conclusion

RLUIPA reflects the current dynamic social, political, and legal environment regarding the role of religion in our society in the context of potential conflicts between churches and land use regulations. Congress has attempted to empower churches when they choose where and how they build a sanctuary or assemble for worship, and to restrain local governments when they seek to apply zoning or landmark regulations to those churches. Local governments face a difficult task seeking to avoid RLUIPA claims and evaluating the likelihood of such claims prevailing, if challenged. However, local officials can take many steps to lessen the likelihood of a potential claim, including: a comprehensive review of the treatment of religious institutions in its land use codes, both substantively and procedurally, training officials and employees to be sensitive to religious differences, and recognizing that land use applications from—and enforcement of regulations against—religious institutions must be handled with special care.

Notes

1. 146 CONG. REC. S7774 (daily ed. July 27, 2000) (joint statement of Sens. Kennedy and Hatch).
2. While RLUIPA claims have fared somewhat better than religious use claims prior to RLUIPA (*see, e.g.*, Note, *Religious Land Use in the Federal Courts Under RLUIPA*, 120 HARV. L. REV. 2178 (2007)), local governments have prevailed in a substantial proportion of all RLUIPA litigation.
3. Interior designation, because it "freezes" the interior at a point in time and thus would disallow changes to reflect subsequent doctrinal developments, may readily be seen either as imposing a substantial burden on religious exercise or violating the establishment clause; *see, e.g., Soc'y of Jesus v. Boston Landmarks Comm'n*, 409 Mass. 38 (1990).
4. *See generally* Alan C. Weinstein, *The Myth of Ministry vs. Mortar: A Legal and Policy Analysis of Landmark Designation of Religious Institutions*, 65 TEMP. L. REV. 91 (1992).
5. *See, e.g., Hollywood Cmty. Synagogue, Inc. v. City of Hollywood, Fla.*, 436 F. Supp. 2d 1325 (S.D. Fla. 2006) (granting exceptions to day care and education centers, but denying exception to house of worship, violated RLUIPA). In that case, after losing a RLUIPA challenge, city officials agreed to a settlement that included paying $2 million to the RLUIPA plaintiff and agreed that city employees, including elected officials, would attend mandatory religious sensitivity training. *See* Todd Wright, *Hollywood to Pay $2 Million to Synagogue*, MIAMI HERALD ONLINE, June 26, 2006, 2006 WLNR 11054024.

6. *See, e.g., Lighthouse Cmty. Church of God v. City of Southfield et al.*, 2007 WL 30280 (E.D. Mich. 2007) (disputing views of whether city officials ever represented to church that a property could be used for religious purposes).
7. 436 F. Supp. 2d 1325 (S.D. Fla. 2006).
8. Note, *supra* note 2.
9. *See Castle Hills First Baptist Church of God v. City of Castle Hills*, 2004 WL 546792 (W.D. Tex. 2004).
10. *See St. John's United Church of Christ v. City of Chicago*, 502 F.3d 616 (7th Cir. 2007), *aff'g* 401 F. Supp. 2d 887 (N.D. Ill. 2005). Here, the Seventh Circuit held that eminent domain was not a land use regulation, listed other cases in accord, and noted that the only exception was dicta in an early RLUIPA case, *Cottonwood Christian Ctr. v. Cypress Redevelopment Agency*, 218 F. Supp. 2d 1203, 1222 n.9 (C.D. Cal. 2002).
11. *Vision Church, United Methodist v. Vill. of Long Grove*, 468 F.3d 975 (7th Cir. 2006).
12. *Prater v. City of Burnside, Ky.*, 289 F.3d 417 (6th Cir. 2002).
13. *Taylor v. City of Gary, Ind.*, 2007 WL 1317130 (7th Cir. 2007).
14. *Omnipoint Commc'ns, Inc. v. City of White Plains*, 202 F.R.D. 402 (S.D.N.Y. 2001).
15. *See, e.g., Midrash Sephardi, Inc. v. Town of Surfside*, 366 F.3d 1214, 1229 (11th Cir. 2004).
16. *See, e.g., Guru Nanak Sikh Soc'y of Yuba City v. Sutter County*, 456 F.3d 978, 986 (9th Cir. 2006) (stating "RLUIPA applies when the government may take into account the particular details of an applicant's proposed use of land when deciding to permit or deny that use"). One recent case argues that enforcement actions triggered by citizen complaints can also constitute an "individualized assessment." In that case, the city had enacted an ordinance restricting parking in residential districts, enforcement of which was triggered when the city received written complaints from three individuals residing in three separate households within 1,500 feet of the property where the parking violation was alleged to have occurred. When enforcement was sought against a rectory located in a residential district, the court ruled that this exclusive delegation of enforcement authority constituted a subjective system of individualized

assessment, because enforcement was not uniform but was left entirely to the whim of any three individuals who met the necessary criteria. *See Town of Foxfield v. Archdiocese of Denver*, 148 P.3d 339 (Colo. App. 2006).

17. *See, e.g., Sts. Constantine & Helen Greek Orthodox Church, Inc. v. City of New Berlin*, 396 F.3d 895 (7th Cir. 2005) (finding denial of rezoning application to violate RLUIPA).
18. *See, Greater Bible Way Temple of Jackson v. City of Jackson*, 487 Mich. 373 (Mich. 2007).
19. *See, e.g., Cottonwood Christian Ctr. v. Cypress Redevelopment Agency*, 218 F. Supp. 2d 1203, 1221 (C.D. Cal. 2002) ("Church activities have a significant impact on interstate commerce.").
20. *See, e.g., Guru Nanak Sikh Soc'y*, 456 F.3d 978; *Elsinore Christian Ctr. v. City of Lake Elsinore*, 197 Fed. Appx. 718; *Sts. Constantine & Helen Greek Orthodox Church, Inc.*, 396 F.3d 895; *DiLaura v. Twp. of Ann Arbor*, 112 Fed. Appx. 445 (6th Cir. 2004) (per curiam); *Living Water Church of God v. Charter Twp. of Meridian*, 384 F. Supp. 2d 1123 (W.D. Mich. 2005); *Castle Hills First Baptist Church v. City of Castle Hills*, 2004 WL 546792.
21. *See Civil Liberties for Urban Believers v. City of Chicago*, 342 F.3d 752 (7th Cir. 2003); *see also Vision Church, United Methodist v. Vill. of Long Grove*, 468 F.3d 975; *Petra Presbyterian Church v. Vill. of Northbrook*, 489 F.3d 846 (7th Cir. 2007).
22. *Sts. Constantine & Helen Greek Orthodox Church, Inc.*, 396 F.3d 895.
23. *See Midrash Sephardi, Inc. v. Town of Surfside*, 366 F.3d 1214. However, that court also found that the ban violated RLUIPA's equal terms provision. *Id.*
24. *Elsinore Christian Ctr.*, 197 Fed. Appx. 718, *rev'g on other grounds* 291 F. Supp. 2d 1083 (C.D. Cal. 2003).
25. *Midrash Sephardi, Inc.*, 366 F.3d 1214.
26. *Murphy v. Zoning Comm'n of Town of New Milford*, 148 F. Supp. 2d 173, 191 (D. Conn. 2001), *vacated on ripeness grounds*, 402 F.3d 342 (2d Cir. 2005).

9

RLUIPA and Planners: The Importance of Fairness in Planning for and Regulating Religious Land Uses

Graham S. Billingsley, AICP

There is one basic rule when dealing with religious land use applicants: be fair, be very fair. Be sure the rules are clear and that you treat them the same as other similar uses. Land use decisions about churches and other religious uses should be based exclusively on the impacts of the use, not on the religious nature. If there is any hint of inconsistency in treatment between a religious use and another institutional or commercial use, the community—having made a sound land use decision—may find itself having to justify that decision to a court.

Institutional uses are critical to a community. At the same time, planners will tell you they can have very big land use impacts. Schools, churches, day care centers, cemeteries, group homes—all these religious and secular uses exist in every community. Several of these are commonly found in residential neighborhoods, particularly schools and churches. Elementary schools are generally encouraged to locate in residential areas: the areas they serve. Churches traditionally have been located within, or immediately adjacent to, residential neighborhoods as well. High schools, on the other hand, are more commonly sited on arterials—perhaps near a residential neighborhood, but not in it. This is logical because the catchment area for a high school is usually much larger than a single residential neighborhood, and because of the associated traffic, noise, night activities, and other characteristics.

Everyone has a mental picture of what institutional uses look like, but such images may be outdated. In many places, schools no longer are sized and located for easy access by students of all ages; most churches are no longer in use on Sundays only. School board budgets and more expansive views of a church's mission mean these uses are very different today than their historic, Norman Rockwell stereotype.

Changes often come as a surprise to communities. The private school approved a few years ago for 120 students has become very popular and now wants to expand to three hundred, with thoughts of becoming even bigger by adding a high school, large gymnasium, and other buildings. The church built with seed money from a church thirty miles away started small with one Sunday service and some community activities. The development of the community adds significantly to the congregation, and the church may wish to expand. Its leaders want to add a school, community meeting rooms, and a new chapel for smaller weddings and baptisms because the main sanctuary has become very busy with multiple services and requests for big weddings. The church may have been five thousand square feet, then expanded to twenty thousand square feet, and now wants to triple in size. Traffic was insignificant with the original building, but now will require road improvements for safe access.

Another source of land use conflict and concern for planners and their communities is the religious assembly that is not connected to a traditional church: the prayer meetings in a living room; the tent set up for the weekend for a visiting preacher. These uses are often unexpected and unplanned for, and can impact neighbors. This story is played out every week throughout the country.

How can a community show it has treated religious use applicants fairly? Good planning requires good plans. Does the comprehensive plan consider institutional uses in anything more than a cursory way? When was it developed, and does it address churches as they are today—from "mega churches" to home-based worship, or only an idealized older concept like the steeple church on the village green? Most comprehensive plans include community institutional uses, but few really address land use implications, the full range of potential sizes, and the extent of these uses. The potential land use impacts have to be planned for to ensure that such uses fit the community's goals for growth and development. That's just good planning—which should be the basis for every land use decision.

All effective comprehensive plans have goals and policies that reflect the desire of the community. The plan is usually not specific—that's left to the regulations, but the plan can't be so vague that it lacks clear direction for staff and the decision makers. What is the image the community wants? How will services be delivered to the community? Policies on religious institutions should be included for other community uses such as parks, schools, nursing homes, and day care.

Identifying and planning for neighborhood character is critical if the community desires to limit the size and impacts of institutional uses. Possible goals and policies related to institutional uses could include descriptions of neighborhoods that address level of traffic, size of structures, types of uses, and relationships to the larger community and centralized services. Although each community's goals and policies must flow from the local public planning processes used in the preparation or update of its comprehensive plan, a few examples of such goals and policies illustrate the importance of identifying neighborhood character.

These examples come from Monterey, California[1], and Boulder County, Colorado.[2]

California

Goal: New development should be sensitive to its immediate surrounding neighborhood. An important attraction of this community is the existence of separate and distinct residential neighborhoods. Each is unique and different from the others. New development should respond to the predominate features that define a neighborhood and reinforce them. Neighborhood compatibility standards recognize that conformance with individual site design or architectural guidelines does not assure that neighborhood compatibility is achieved.

Policy: The design of new buildings should recognize the site, building and landscape characteristics including size and intensity of use that define neighborhood character and incorporate them into the design.

Guideline: A neighborhood is primarily defined as that area of the city that is visually impacted by the building project. This will normally include the street frontage between adjacent cross streets, properties along that frontage and properties located within the same block as that of the building project.

Guideline: Designers are responsible for identifying the predominant features in a neighborhood that establish that neighborhood's character and include those characteristics in the building proposed. Physical features which often provide clues to neighborhood character include:

1. What is the distance or separation between adjacent buildings?
2. How many garages or open parking spaces are typical?
3. What type of landscaping is predominantly visible to the street?
4. Are the front yards open or enclosed in fences or hedges?
5. Does one particular roof shape dominate?
6. Is there a predominant building material?
7. Is there a predominance of single-story or two-story profiles at the street?
8. Is there a predominant color theme?

Colorado

Policy: Based upon past and present land use, lack of community services, physical conditions, and citizen desires, it is county policy to recognize and designate the existing land use character as being agricultural in nature and to ensure that the accompanying Land Use Plan Map and attendant Land Use Code will acknowledge such character in the designation and implementation of future land use types.

1. Business uses that are primarily oriented to the local community or otherwise complement the "semi-rural" character;
2. The existence of internal open space that serves to physically separate nonagricultural land uses;
3. An ultimate geographic size that acts to physically contain the community, enhance community identity, and prevent development "sprawl" into the surrounding agricultural lands;
4. The existence of external open space (agricultural land) that is contiguous to the ultimate developmental peripheries of the community.

Policy: It shall be county policy to maintain the "semi-rural" character and the maximum overall gross density of the rural community and to maximize open space in and around future developments. In addition, new developments planned adjacent to existing developments and within the same zoning district shall reflect the general density and design characteristics of the existing developments.

The details needed to implement the goals and policies in the comprehensive plan are defined in the zoning code and other land use regulations. These, along with the plan itself, should be kept up to date. Do they account for recent changes to the comprehensive plan? Do they reflect changes in state or federal law or recent court cases?

Addressing religious uses in the zoning code is critical. The land use regulations have to be logical with distinctions clearly defined. Definitions are a particular concern. Many codes simply have a basic definition of religious use. These definitions can seem very broad and straightforward, such as "a place for public worship." Or they may be more specific, such as: "Church—An establishment, the principal purpose of which is religious worship, and for which the principal building or other structure contains the sanctuary or principal place of worship, and which includes related accessory uses." Either approach may be insufficient to give clarity, with respect to how particular religious uses should be treated. The broad definition might seem to exclude places for nonworship religious functions. The more specific one for a "church" would not provide guidance as to non-church-related religious activities. Were these definitions developed with the potential of today's religious uses? Too often, communities conceive of religious activity in terms of the formal structure of the mainstream, dominant religions. Failing to address other forms of religious activities, such as prayer meetings, Native American ritual celebrations, and nonworship activities leaves communities vulnerable. The zoning code must be capable of accommodating all possible forms of religious practice. If the definition can be construed as excluding or prohibiting certain religious uses altogether, then the definition needs to be changed.

The *Planners Dictionary* distinguishes between "church," "community church," "large church," "megachurch," neighborhood church," "small church," "religious assembly," "religious institution," and "religious retreat."[3]

The following definition attempts to address all possible uses of a religious facility:

> Facilities operated by religious organizations for worship, or the promotion of religious activities, including churches, mosques, synagogues, temples, etc.; and accessory uses on the same site, including living quarters for ministers and staff, child day care facilities and religious schools where authorized by the same type of land use permit required for the religious facility itself. Religious facilities may also include emergency shelters, and fund raising sales, bazaars, dinners, parties, or other outdoor events on the same site. Other establishments maintained by religious organizations, including full time educational institutions, hospitals and other potentially related operations (for example, a recreational camp) are classified according to their respective activities.[4]

This definition seems to cover almost all possible religious uses if one assumes that prayer meetings are covered by "the promotion of religious activities." Adding a specific reference to prayer meetings and other group rites, or rituals conducted outside of a religious facility, might be better. However, it is easy to see how cumbersome such a definition can be and to envision that there might be other activities that have been overlooked.

Religious uses can be allowed in all districts, or only in some. However, they must be allowed in the same districts as other, similar institutional uses. A community might have a district that just doesn't make sense for institutional uses, for example, a heavy industrial district. If the comprehensive plan is the blueprint for a community, and industrial uses are important to that plan, why would a community want to allow institutional uses such as a church to take up any of the limited area available for that valuable industrial use? It isn't easy to zone new industrial land within a community. To place it outside, or on the edge, creates a traffic-related sprawl problem in most cases. To try to zone land industrial next to existing nonindustrial areas is a nightmare most planners would prefer to avoid. Other zoning districts might exclude institutional uses such as districts for forestry or agriculture, and special overlay districts (such as conservation or historic districts) that do not have religious uses at the time of creation. Remember—if religious uses are excluded from a district, then all nonreligious uses of similar type should be excluded.

Churches may be allowed by right in any district, but if so, other similar institutional uses also have to be allowed by right. If there is a desire to have their development plans reviewed, then the same local review process that applies to other institutional applicants should apply to religious land use applicants. An exception is an overriding state law limiting local review for a particular type of use, as exists for public schools in some places. In that case, make certain that all other institutional uses are treated no more or less favorably than similar religious uses. A common approach is to base the review on impact, so if any use exceeds a certain traffic level, number of parking spaces, number of people, or a certain size, then review is required regardless of type of use. This ensures a level and fair playing field for all. A couple of examples of threshold regulations illustrate this point. The first is from Boulder County, Colorado,[5] and the second from Oakland, California.[6]

Special review is required for any use which:

a. generates traffic volumes in excess of 150 average daily trips per lot, as defined by the Institute of Transportation Engineers;
b. has an occupant load greater than or equal to 100 persons per lot;
c. has a wastewater flow greater than or equal to 2,000 gallons per day per lot;
d. has a total floor area greater than 25,000 square feet; or
e. has a second principal use which does not increase density.

Any project that meets any of the following size thresholds:

a. The actual project site (including only portions of the lot actually affected by the project) exceeds one acre;
b. Nonresidential projects involving twenty-five thousand (25,000) square feet or more of floor area, except in the R-80, R-90, C-51, C-55, S-2, or S-15 zones;
c. Residential projects requiring a conditional use permit for density resulting in a total number of dwelling units as follows:
    i. Two or more dwelling units in the R-35 zone, except in the case of a Secondary Unit,
    ii. Three or more dwelling units in the R-36 or R-40 zone,
    iii. Seven or more dwelling units in the R-50 zone.
d. Residential projects requiring a conditional use permit to exceed the basic or permitted density resulting in seven or more dwelling units in the R-60, R-70, R-80, or R-90 zone.
e. Large Scale Developments. Any development which is located in the R-80, R-90, C-51, C-55, S-2, or S-15 zone and results in more than one hundred thousand (100,000) square feet of new floor area, or a new building, or portion thereof, of more than one hundred twenty (120) feet in height.

Review processes need to be straightforward and uniform for all similar uses. One might argue that frustration resulting from an onerous application and review process might deliberately discourage or deny a religious use, and make a community vulnerable by giving the appearance of unfair treatment. Bureaucracy may be necessary to a point because formal review processes assure objective, even-handed treatment. But review processes can build incrementally over time as they are amended to deal first with one particular issue and then another, so that they reach a level of complexity that makes it difficult for applicants. Ensure that the triggers for special or conditional uses are reasonably related to the potential impacts. It is much better to have clear, objective thresholds, such as level of traffic, than a subjective trigger such as "greater than expected impact to a neighborhood."

Even with a good plan and a clear set of zoning regulations, some applications (and applicants) will test the staff and decision makers. The simpler and clearer the regulations are, the better. Even similar land uses tend to have different impacts depending on where they are proposed. If the community has a variety of natural features, history, neighborhoods, and other relevant characteristics, the regulations need to account for these differences. This tends to lead to regulations with more subjective components. Subjective standards can be acceptable, as long as they are interpreted and administered in a consistent way for all applicants.

At minimum, regulations should include review standards for traffic, noise, size, and environmental impacts. In addition, neighborhood compatibility standards are very helpful if the community wishes to make decisions that account for the unique aspects of each application and location.

What has been the history of reviews and approvals? How have institutional uses been treated in the past by the planning commission or council? How have religious uses been treated? Hopefully there has been consistency in the decisions approving or denying development approvals for religious and other institutional uses. Consistency doesn't mean that churches or other institutional uses are always approved or always denied; rather, that from an objective viewpoint the standards have been applied consistently, and that any differences in outcome can be seen as attributable to salient differences between the uses or the locations at which they are proposed. For example, if there is a standard regarding traffic level of service (LOS) that requires all development not to degrade that LOS, then all projects that do degrade the LOS should be denied. If there is a history of project approval even when the

LOS is degraded, then it will be difficult to avoid being challenged over a denial that is based, even in part, on LOS degradation.

If reviews have not historically been as consistent as they should be, it is advisable to provide training for the planning commission, zoning board of review, and city council or county commissioners. This training should cover general procedures, processes, rules against ex parte communication, and other relevant concerns, and should include specific training on legal implications of the decision makers' actions. One of the best forms of training is a review of legal cases that have relevance to the community and the issues it faces. There are a large number of religious land use cases that address a variety of different issues related to the application and interpretation of RLUIPA.

What happens if you have a change on the city council or planning commission and the new board wants to go in a different policy direction from its predecessor? In that case it is usually better to amend the existing regulations rather than to change standing interpretations of the existing regulations. Depending on the circumstances, a court may not care that the most recent interpretation came from a different group of people than the ones who made previous decisions that are arguably inconsistent. This will also give an opportunity for additional education about the existing comprehensive plan and zoning regulations.

So, you've taken a look at your regulations, and your history of decisions and interpretations and know that you need to make changes. What fun! I was in Dallas when the city decided that churches should be reviewed for impacts. So many churches were upset by this decision that the first (and last) public meeting was held in the convention center to accommodate the crowds. This is, of course, an elected official's biggest nightmare. It is not a lot of fun for planners either.

Generally, the best time to take on difficult issues is prior to the application that polarizes the community. Working on neighborhood compatibility goals and policies in the comprehensive plan brings together the neighborhoods and the institutional uses and commercial uses, and usually leads to productive dialogue and a thorough understanding of the issues by all, which then builds a foundation for changes in the land use code.

If the changes to the land use code stem from community work to develop the basis for those changes in the comprehensive plan, then less education is needed, and the general purposes of the regulations are better understood by all. This reduces the discussion to the question of the best way to write the regulations, instead of whether new regulations should be written at all. Of course, this never works perfectly. There are always people who don't get involved at the start, or who did get involved but never agreed to the policies approved by consensus of the community. These days, the internet is invaluable. Even though there are still many people without access, many more do and can follow the progress of the planning and regulatory revision process.

People tend to want to avoid conflict. This is just as true for planners and elected officials as it is for everyone else, if not more so. If the intent is to keep large institutional uses out of neighborhoods, then that needs to be stated up front. If, instead, it is hidden in a general neighborhood compatibility exercise that is unclear, or includes vague policies or weak standards when an actual proposal faces the community, the initial exercise will have been for naught and, in fact, could actually make the review process more difficult. If the intent is to allow large churches in the community, it is just as important that citizens know that.

In conclusion, when faced with a question about how to handle an application concerning a religious use, above all else remember the rule at the beginning of this chapter—be fair, be very, very fair.

Notes

1. Monterey, Cal., Architectural Review Committee, Neighborhood Compatibility Design Guidelines, ARC Res. 92-04 (1992), *available at* http://www.monterey.org/planningengineering/arc/neigh_compat.html.
2. Boulder County, Colo., Boulder County Comprehensive Plan (1978), *available at* http://www.bouldercounty.org/lu/bccp/ (last visited Mar. 19, 2009).
3. A Planners Dictionary, PAS Report No. 521/522 (2004).

4. South Pasadena, Cal., Municipal Code ch. 36, art. 7, div. 36.7 (2009), *available at* http://www.qcode.us/codes/southpasadena.
5. Boulder, Colo., Land Use Code art. 4 (2009), *available at* http://www.co.boulder.co.us/lu/lucode/pdf/Boulder_County_Land_Use_Code_Article_4.pdf (last visited Mar. 19, 2009).
6. Oakland, Cal., Municipal Code ch. 17, §136, *available at* http://municipalcodes.lexisnexis.com/codes/oakland/ (last visited Mar. 19, 2009).

10 The Top Ten Tips

Daniel P. Dalton, Vivian Kahn, FAICP,
and Bryan W. Wenter, AICP

Cheat sheets are always helpful—the "to do" lists the lawyer or planner keeps in his or her back pocket as a reminder of what's important and what not to forget. There are three such lists included in this chapter—one for each of the major participants in the RLUIPA dance—prepared by experienced RLUIPA practitioners. The first list is for the religious land use applicant, the second is addressed to the planner, and the final list is one the local government attorney should keep close. Each is a good refresher of many of the points presented in earlier chapters.

The Religious Land Use Applicant

1. Plan for Growth

Many churches approach a community with a plan to address current needs, but a better approach is to have a vision of the church in ten to fifteen years, and plan accordingly. Effective religious organizations grow rapidly. A common problem is planning for an immediate need based on existing financial pressures, leading the church to win the legal battle, but then return to the community to seek relief for future expansion. Always be mindful of your growth plans.

2. Understand the Local Politics, Ordinances, and Master Plan

If a community is "studying the loss of tax base" due to the number of churches within its borders, it may be less likely to grant a favorable site plan review or zoning variance to a religious land use applicant. Local politicians may pressure code enforcement and building officials to "code the building to death" if they do not want the church. Review minutes of the local government's meetings concerning approvals or denials pertaining to religious land use applicants. A church should also review the community's land use ordinances to determine if a church is allowed by right on the property, by special permit, or not at all. If the community's regulations do not allow the church to use the property as of right, be cognizant of the local rules and restrictions. Finally, review the community's master plan to determine the community's "vision for growth." Look at the portions of the master plan that address studies of traffic patterns, subdivision development, future needs for public facilities, population trends, employment trends, preservation of open space, and the like to determine what the community anticipates for religious land uses in the future.

3. Address the Community's Concerns Promptly

Address traffic, parking, building code compliance, noise, and other neighbor concerns; use an appraiser to demonstrate that the value of residential property increases when the church is nearby. A religious land use applicant should be sensitive to its neighbors. It is good practice to host an informational meeting with neighbors explaining what the proposed use is, what will occur on the premises, and how it might affect them before the development plans are submitted to the community. In addition to concerns about traffic, neighbors may oppose a new church because of noise and a decrease in property values. A church can obviate noise objections by agreeing not to use outdoor prayer calls, bells, and chimes, and by complying with requirements for setbacks and minimum lot size.

4. Define the Religious Exercise Sought by the Church

Community officials might attack a proposed religious land use by finding that the use is not a legitimate religious exercise. A church should educate the community about what it intends to do with the property, including anticipated accessory uses and activities. Many religious land use applicants make much more intensive use of their buildings than in years past. Be prepared to explain how the proposed land uses are central to the applicant's religious beliefs and practices.

5. Keep Detailed Records

Statements made during a meeting or public hearing and what may constitute the public record for purposes of litigation are two different things. When meeting with city planners informally, the religious land use applicant should keep a detailed record of what is said, what is agreed upon, and what needs to be done. Remember—the record can be in the form of letters "confirming our conversation," detailed minutes, or a memorandum setting forth the date, time, participants of the meeting, the topics of discussion, and the agreed-upon points. During the formal meetings, retain a court reporter to transcribe what is said. It is remarkable how many times the community's video or audio tape machine "malfunctions" during critical hearings. A complete record is important for the lawyer handling the RLUIPA matter, because many times the lawyer is not involved in the early stages of the development review process.

6. Prepare for the Cost of Litigation

The financial costs involved in RLUIPA litigation are unpredictable and expensive, with no real tangible result until the end of the case. The church should request a budget from the legal team and prepare to exceed the budget due to the inherent unpredictability in such cases. There are other costs to be mindful of as well—such as the loss of support and membership in the community and within the church when the lawsuit is filed. The RLUIPA case may drag on for many months or years. Most people seek religion as a refuge from the grind of daily life, not to support lengthy litigation. Prepare for the loss of members, staff, and support in the community.

7. Use the Freedom of Information Act Frequently

A benefit of litigating against a local government is that it must provide documents to a party requesting them under the state's Freedom of Information Act (FOIA) before suit is filed; failure to do so may give rise to a claim under the act. In many cases, the FOIA coordinator does not keep a copy of what is sent out, and the insurance defense attorney retained to represent the community will have no idea what the opponent has. Be sure to ask for electronic mail in the FOIA request. People tend to use e-mail as a conversation as opposed to a form of recording events, which could prove beneficial to the religious land use applicant's case.

8. Retain Experts Early, Before the Lawsuit Is Filed

In order to pursue a claim through trial, the religious land use applicant might need to retain a land use planner, a commercial appraiser, a traffic consultant, a wetlands expert, and a damages expert. Before the lawsuit is filed, have the experts review the case to make sure they have no conflicts and can support the conclusions the religious land use applicant hopes to reach. Consider retaining two of each, just in case one does not support the applicant's position or does not work well with the other experts. Try to have them "trial ready" before the case is filed.

9. Be Prepared for Trial Before Filing the Lawsuit

Once a religious land use applicant is on the path to trial, make certain it has all of the evidence necessary to advance a preliminary injunction claim and rebut a summary judgment motion. Review the state of the law in your local jurisdiction to determine which court would be best for this case. You may find filing in federal court is a better option based on three concerns. First, the federal courts are better equipped to address the substantive claims and handle abusive discovery filings that might be submitted by the insurance defense counsel retained by the community. Second, judges in some states must be reelected, and they rely on local political leaders for support for their reelection campaigns. Federal judges are not subject to the same political pressure. Finally, the religious land use applicant must be able to demonstrate its religious exercise, the individualized assessment, the substantial burden, or the unequal terms before suit is filed.

10. Keep the Spiritual Leader Informed but Separate from the Legal Team

There are two competing interests involved when representing a religious land use applicant. The first is that every member of the church feels that he or she has a personal stake in the case. The other is that every member of the church looks to his or her spiritual leader for answers to the lawsuit. Litigation is complicated, expensive, time consuming, and overwhelming at times. Decisions must be made on a daily basis. Keep the spiritual leader in the loop, but use a group of leaders to be the contact with the law firm. Have available a mechanism such as quarterly meetings to review the performance of the group, and replace those leaders if their decisions do not mesh with the overall goals of the church.

The Community Planner

1. Understand and Appreciate RLUIPA's Scope and Purpose

Every planner should read the provisions of the Religious Land Use and Institutionalized Person's Act.[1] Supreme Court Justice Brennan opined in his dissenting opinion in *San Diego Gas & Electric Co. v. City of San Diego* that planners, like policemen, should know the Constitution; likewise, planners should also know important federal laws that directly impact the work they do.[2] RLUIPA is one such statute. Periodically, sit down with your counsel and refresh one another, and especially new staff members, about RLUIPA's provisions. Remember, for purposes of RLUIPA, a "land use regulation" means a zoning or land marking law and "religious exercise" means any exercise of religion, whether or not compelled by, or central to, a system of religious belief, including the use, building, or conversion of real property for the purpose of religious exercise. 42 U.S.C. §2000cc-5. Religious uses include churches, synagogues, and mosques, but can also include day care facilities, gyms, senior centers, and "social" events celebrating religious rites.

2. *Plan for Religious Land Uses Comprehensively*

Anticipate and plan for the growth and needs of different types of religious land uses as you would for any other institutional use. Respond to requests from religious leaders in the community to discuss their plans and obtain input about the future growth of their congregations. Include religious institutions among the neighborhood groups that are notified about public meetings and workshops when you update your comprehensive plan or land use regulations.

3. *Audit Your Comprehensive Plan and Land Use Regulations*

Ensure that the community's land use plans and regulations provide reasonable and feasible options for new or expanding religious assemblies, as well as accessory uses such as religious schools. Making adequate provision for social services (such as shelters, feeding programs, and facilities for the homeless and indigent) operated by secular organizations as well as government agencies reduces the need for religious institutions to provide such services. Relaxing the rules for location in developed areas can relieve pressure for siting religious assemblies in low density and rural areas with inadequate services. Evaluate ordinances and their implementation to ensure that religious and nonreligious activities with similar operational characteristics are regulated in a similar manner. A problem might arise, for example, in allowing theaters, recreation centers, and lodge halls by right or subject to conditional permit while religious assembly uses require special approval or are prohibited. Carefully review the definitions in your regulations. *A Planners Dictionary* (American Planning Association, PAS Report 521/522, 2004) is a good resource for definitions. At the same time, don't be afraid to regulate different types of religious uses in a different manner based on their land use characteristics. For example, while a religious assembly use may be defined to include Sunday school or day care during services, a parochial school offering a course of instruction that complies with state education requirements for K–12 or a day care center open to the entire community can be regulated in the same manner as a comparable secular private school or day care center.

4. Work with Applicants Early in the Development Review Process

If your community does not have a pre-application process, consider instituting one. Applicants should be encouraged to sit down with city officials to sketch out their plans as early in the development review process as possible before they expend large sums in designing their project. The applicant may be more amenable to adjusting his or her plans early in the process to address issues raised by city officials. First impressions are important; the pre-application process might be the key in establishing a good relationship with the religious land use applicant. Be sure to document the understandings and any agreements from the pre-application process in a letter to the applicant.

5. Ascertain that Design Regulations Do Not Conflict with Religious Values or Traditions

Don't apply design regulations in a manner that may conflict with religious values or traditions regarding features such as onion domes, minarets, and steeples.

6. Incorporate Strong Findings in the Record

Findings should explain why the decision:

- does not constitute a *substantial burden* that limits religious practice;
- is necessary to serve *compelling* governmental interest, and
- is the *least restrictive* means for furthering that interest.

Individualized determinations (decisions on use permits and variances) that limit religious uses must be supported by evidence showing a *compelling* governmental interest. The typical "public purpose" finding required for such determinations is probably not a sufficient basis for regulating religious activity. Don't be afraid to make a distinction between a religious practice and a nuisance (for example, massive holiday displays with amplified music, excessively bright lights, noncompliance with accessibility requirements). Offer and document the feasibility of alternative approaches to the design and operation of the religious land use (for example, different parking arrangements and design options). The record should document the availability of reasonable alternatives but ought to consider the actual availability of alternate locations and the economics of the religious organization.

7. Treat Every Land Use Applicant Fairly

It goes without saying that all land use applicants must be treated fairly in the development review process. Religious land use applicants are no different. Treat the minority denominations and their facilities (e.g., mosques, fundamentalist sects) on the same basis as mainstream denominations. This may require education of decision makers to ensure that their actions cannot be construed as discriminatory based on comments in the record.

8. Don't Unduly Burden Religious Practices

Watch for regulations and requirements that might limit or "burden" religious practice by restricting the number of worshippers or hours of operation, or requiring special permits. Application of zoning regulations in a neutral manner to religious and nonreligious uses alike might not validate a local decision if the church can argue that the regulation imposes a substantial burden. Planners may liken this requirement to the reasonable accommodation requirements of the Fair Housing Act.

9. Provide Alternate Means of Relief

Provide alternate means of relief from regulatory requirements to avoid the need for variances. Such regulatory schemes could include granting waivers or exceptions to allow reasonable accommodation, based on a finding that the use is entitled to protection under RLUIPA. The granting of relief can be conditioned to apply only to the specific grantee or to a successor entitled to the same protection.

10. Hold Practice Sessions

Periodically organize a practice session with your local counsel that provides a "dry run" for elected officials, appointed commissioners, and staff to respond to challenging scenarios, such as a religious land use applicant. Be sure to include a post-critique of the scenario in order to provide constructive criticism and guidance, especially for new officials and staff.

The Local Government Lawyer

1. Understand RLUIPA's Scope and Applicability

Understand the scope and limits of RLUIPA. Just because a governmental decision may affect a religious land use applicant, it does not necessarily mean that the decision impermissibly burdens religious exercise. Remember that just as purely secular activities are not protected, not every activity undertaken by a religious institution constitutes religious exercise.

2. Understand the Nature and Risks of RLUIPA Litigation

RLUIPA elevates religious discrimination claims to the level of federal civil rights violations, and it eliminates the presumption of validity traditionally provided to the legislative decisions of local government officials in land use and zoning matters. RLUIPA may be enforced by the U.S. Department of Justice and, under federal civil rights laws, RLUIPA liability may be accompanied by significant monetary awards. Local governments should recognize, however, that RLUIPA does not exempt religious organizations from land use regulations. Consequently, even in the face of RLUIPA litigation, municipalities and counties should not disregard their own zoning requirements when there is no finding that a federal law has been or would be violated.

3. Avoid RLUIPA Lawsuits

Conflict over the application of land use regulations and religious facilities has increased in recent years, in part as a result of the adoption of RLUIPA. While some of the tension is perhaps inevitable, due to the larger size and more intense use of such facilities, the risk of RLUIPA lawsuits can be minimized or avoided. Local governments should carefully analyze their land use regulations, and change any policies or practices that impose a substantial burden on religious exercise. It is important to ensure that land use regulations allow reasonable opportunities for expanding or constructing new religious facilities and accessory religious uses. It is also important to create exceptions from such policies or practices where they otherwise would substantially burden religious exercise. Such an approach will ensure that additional processes are available for potential RLUIPA plaintiffs to exhaust so that a RLUIPA lawsuit might be avoided.

4. Review Applications

Local government attorneys should carefully review applications for religious land uses with staff planners to ensure that land use permitting requirements do not single out religious institutions and practices, and are reasonably related to the potential impacts of the proposed use. However, as with any other use, applicants for religious land uses must comply with basic application requirements that do not create a substantial burden on religion.

5. Consider Potential Discrimination Issues

Be aware of (and sensitive to) potential claims alleging that a given governmental action impermissibly discriminates against the exercise of religion. Advise government officials and staff charged with the implementation and interpretation of comprehensive plans and zoning ordinances that any individualized governmental decision relating to land use affecting the religious exercise of an individual or institution might be challenged under RLUIPA.

Treat all religious institutions the same, and do not single out particular religious institutions or activities for either favorable or unfavorable treatment, regardless of size or denomination. By the same token, applications for religious uses must be treated no differently than similar applications for secular uses. In short, religious uses must be treated the same, both in procedure and substance, as any other land use with comparable size and impacts. Ensure that religious activities are not favored over nonreligious activities, and that less onerous standards are not applied to nonreligious uses in the same zoning districts as religious uses with similar impacts.

6. Incorporate Strong Findings in the Record

Ensure that the administrative record contains substantial evidence to support decisions that affect religious land uses and structures. Communication with religious applicants should be clear, and documented in writing. Findings regarding individualized determinations should explain why a given governmental action: (1) does not substantially burden religious exercise, (2) is necessary to serve a compelling governmental interest, (3) actually furthers the government's interest, and (4) is the least restrictive means of furthering that interest. Findings should also emphasize that government decisions regarding religious activities are based on land use characteristics and impacts. To minimize or avoid RLUIPA liability, the record should document the availability and feasibility of alternative means of addressing the impacts a given religious land use may impose.

7. Educate Staff and Elected Officials

Consider implementing periodic training workshops for government agency staff and elected officials to help them understand RLUIPA and its requirements. Like any other applicant, an applicant for religious land use should be treated respectfully and fairly. Assume that a religious land use applicant's beliefs are valid. Sensitivity training should serve as a reminder to staff and officials that their comments and decision making process should focus solely on land use and planning issues.

8. Consider Mediating RLUIPA Disputes

Because a RLUIPA case is likely to be filled with emotion, a face-to-face interaction between the interested parties might be the best opportunity to address issues in a respectful setting, and with reasoned discourse. In such a setting, the parties will be best able to understand each other's concerns and positions, and to reach agreement or compromise short of costly and time-consuming litigation.

9. Implement a Records-Retention Policy

Local governments should carefully apply any records-retention policy to applications for religious land uses. A records policy that includes electronic records and e-mail should be developed and implemented if the local government does not already have one.

10. Require Full Mutual Releases Before Settlement

No settlement or partial settlement should be agreed to unless there is a full mutual release of all liability, including attorneys' fees. At the same time, take care that settlement agreements comply with statutory requirements for public notice and review.

Notes

1. 42 U.S.C. §§ 2000cc et seq., *available at* http://www.usdoj.gov/crt/housing/rluipaexplain.htm.
2. 450 U.S. 621, 661 n.26 (1981) (Brennan, J., dissenting).

Conclusion: Seeing the Light through RLUIPA's Haze

Patricia E. Salkin

The preceding chapters provide an excellent overview of the constitutional underpinnings and legislative history of the Religious Land Use and Institutionalized Persons Act (RLUIPA). Admittedly, the law is not perfect. As one chapter author reports, the law represents a compromise between many competing points of view. Religious discrimination should not be tolerated—not in terms of speech, not in terms of right to assemble, and not in terms of exercise of religious beliefs. Whether in school, at work, at home, or in public or private venues—individuals and groups are entitled to be free from religious discrimination.

On balance, governments across the United States do a good job of conducting business in accordance with the First Amendment guarantees that serve to protect religious exercise. There are infrequent instances, however, when one or more government actors let their personal animus overtake their public role, and there are a handful of documented instances of government decision making motivated by proven intentional religious discrimination. The question is: does a law with the strength of RLUIPA, designed to protect religious exercise throughout towns, cities, and villages, go beyond existing constitutional guarantees? Is the magnitude of RLUIPA's impact on community planning justified, based on the limited documented instances of discrimination in land use decision making?

Many supporters and critics carved out their positions prior to the enactment of RLUIPA, during the legislative debates, and now through litigation, scholarship, and other advocacy opportunities. The following discussion presents a likely scenario of how governments, religious groups, and advocates will deal with RLUIPA in the years to come.

RLUIPA and the Executive Branch

There have been many calls for various reforms to RLUIPA, including pleas for repeal by municipal officials[1] and calls for amendments to clarify various vague and undefined provisions. In addition, at least one leading scholar has called upon the Obama administration to seriously reconsider the act, arguing that it has failed to accomplish its intended goals and that significant considerations regarding its impact on communities may have been overlooked in the haste to enact the law.[2] Absent current empirical studies and reports disproving the scant information Congress relied upon when it passed RLUIPA in 2000, and documenting the devastating financial, environmental, and community planning effects of a law that may be an imperfect solution to no existing compelling problem, it is unlikely that Congress (and the White House) will either repeal or overhaul a statute believed to further a constitutionally protected freedom. It is interesting to note that the administration's new director of the White House Domestic Policy Committee worked on the drafting and negotiation of RLUIPA while she was a member of Senator Ted Kennedy's staff.[3] Her insights into the developments leading up to the law, as well as any feedback that might have been received post-enactment, could prove helpful to the administration should they choose to evaluate potential modifications.

RLUIPA and the Judicial Branch

It is unconstitutional to discriminate on the basis of religion. Pure and simple, the Constitution and federal and state statutes make this clear. It is also unconstitutional for the government to favor religion over nonreligion, but most courts have held that RLUIPA does not do this.

The U.S. Supreme Court is unlikely to find the statute unconstitutional. Although RLUIPA's critics hold out hope that the Court will invalidate the law as it did with the Religious Freedom Restoration Act (RFRA),[4] as pointed out in chapter 4, the weight of authority on this point suggests otherwise. First, Congress seems to have addressed the Supreme Court's concerns contained in RFRA. Second, reliance on a footnote in *Cutter v. Wilkinson*—the only RLUIPA case to be decided by the Supreme Court—indicating that the decision as to its constitutionality was limited only to the institutionalized persons aspects of the act, provides a false sense of hope that the Court would find otherwise on the religious land use part of the law.[5] Students of the Supreme Court readily explain that the Court will decide cases only on the narrowest of constitutional issues, and the justices will not address issues that are not squarely before them. Thirdly, as to the question of constitutionality, the overwhelming number of circuit courts of appeal and district courts that have had occasion to comment on the constitutionality of RLUIPA have offered the opinion that the act is, in their view, constitutional. While some scholars have offered a contrary view, or at least have provided a potential roadmap for constitutional arguments including federalism violations, it remains unlikely that the Supreme Court will invalidate the statute.

The Debate Over What Constitutes Religion

Governments and courts in the United States are loath to define exactly what constitutes a religion, possibly for fear of acknowledging the legitimacy of certain religious beliefs while indicating that certain (perhaps minority) beliefs are not legitimate. As a result, courts often skirt the issue by identifying a set of core tenets of faith and ceremonies that, taken together, comprise religious exercise. This somewhat flexible approach for defining religion for the purpose of religious exercise may present a further unintended impact of RLUIPA, as savvy individuals have claimed to be organized religions, including the Apostles of O'Neil[6] (a group of college students living together) and the Church of Universal Love and Music[7] (a group devoted to outdoor music concerts), as a strategy to attempt to avoid local land use regulation through application of RLUIPA provisions to their proposed projects. While the courts are unlikely to begin holding certain faiths to be essentially nonreligious in nature as they continue to explore the interpretation of RLUIPA, they may develop tests to more seriously gauge the sincerity of litigants' religious beliefs.

The religious community could be helpful if it would support clarity in this regard, and denounce attempts by those feigning the existence of a religion for the purpose of bullying local governments into forgoing application of legitimate land use regulations—using RLUIPA as a sword.

Resolving RLUIPA's Lack of Statutory Definitions

As demonstrated by the authors of the preceding pages, RLUIPA is not an example of the finest statutory drafting. Congress dodged the issue of what constitutes religious exercise for purposes of statutory protection. Was the statute intended to protect only houses of worship and schools—as these uses are typically accepted as religious exercises—or are all types of auxiliary uses included in the definition, even those such as banks, offices, gymnasiums, senior housing, affordable housing, drug treatment programs, and food pantries?

Congress also neglected to define key terms in the law, such as what constitutes a "substantial burden" on the exercise of religion, and what constitutes a "compelling governmental interest." Further clarification on what exactly should be considered a "land use regulation" for purposes of the act could be specified (*e.g.*, in addition to zoning, subdivision, and site plan regulations, which are widely accepted as covered, courts are grappling with the act's application to condemnation proceedings and open space plans). These essential phrases have now been left to the courts to interpret and apply, creating a lack of uniformity in application of this national statute.

The legislative arena is typically the fairest forum for these issues to be discussed, debated, and decided, because congressional committees, hearings, and debates provide opportunities for the broadest cross section of citizens to have meaningful input into the lawmaking process. As Professor Hamilton noted in chapter 2, it seems as though municipal interests were not permitted to provide testimony on the record. This is a manipulation of the legislative process that must not be permitted to occur again. The bottom line is, however, absent the political will supported by a groundswell of demand for reexamination of the statute; this vehicle for reform is unlikely.

Advocates must rely on the only other avenue for clarification—the judicial system—for reasoned interpretation and application of seemingly vague terms and standards. Relying on the judicial approach, however, will take a long time and provide unequal results from state to state in both the state and federal court arenas—until the federal circuit courts and, ultimately, the Supreme Court rule on each of the undefined terms.

Leveling the Playing Field

Planning, zoning, and other land use regulations are legitimate constitutional exercises of the police power,[8] and RLUIPA does not state explicitly, nor suggest implicitly, otherwise. Too often stories relayed by municipal officials begin with statements that the applicant, a religious group, threatened to take the municipality to court under RLUIPA if their project was not approved, with all the costs and inconveniences that litigation entails.

Municipalities are further taken aback when it is disclosed that some of these applicants have the support of well known national legal advocacy organizations that are poised to litigate on behalf of the religious applicant,[9] including the United States Department of Justice, which, as pointed out in chapter 5, employs an attorney as "Special Counsel for Religious Discrimination." The playing field must be leveled, as the perception from the municipal point of view is that it is not. Local governments, particularly in challenging economic times, might lack the financial resources necessary to adequately defend frivolous lawsuits through sometimes long and painful litigation. Anecdotally, this has led many municipalities to compromise legitimate community planning goals and regulations out of fear of litigation, acting to quickly approve some applications from religious entities that might have otherwise undergone more careful review that could have resulted in mitigation measures, project modifications, or legitimate denials.

This is not good for neighborhoods, for communities, or for the legitimacy of planning and land use controls.

Although government officials typically receive training and routine legal counsel to enable them to execute the powers and duties of their offices in accordance with constitutional and statutory mandates, members of the general public may not always act with the same sensitivity and understanding of these laws. It is a routine occurrence for members of the public to attend local meetings where land use decisions are made, and for the public to participate in the required public hearing phase of various applications or during a public comment period set aside by boards. Negative public reaction to all types of land uses—big box retail, power plants, certain religious uses, affordable housing, and manufacturing, to name just a few—should not be automatically transposed to become the unstated beliefs and motivations of the government decision makers.

Next Steps

Community planning advocates must organize themselves and encourage others to conduct independent empirical research that will document and set in context any instances of systemic or infrequent, unique abuse. This information is needed to balance the current allegations of rampant discrimination that led to the enactment of RLUIPA, the magnitude of which, many assert, is exaggerated.

Further, an organized educational effort is needed to supplement the information currently available from the Department of Justice's First Freedom Web site.[10] Municipal officials, planners, and community members must be able to access factual information, explanations of the law, and key phrases and terms, and would benefit from a forum both virtually and in person to communicate ideas, questions, and advice. Practical advice on avoiding RLUIPA claims, such as the information contained in chapters 7, 8, 9, and 10, should be required reading, and easily accessible to all decision makers.

Perhaps a new national organization should be created to help coordinate and facilitate the need for ongoing training and education that has been detailed in the preceding pages. Such an organized effort could provide the sustained leadership necessary to educate lawmakers, policymakers, and the judiciary about various aspects of the law, and the legal rights and needs of all stakeholders—religious groups, municipal governments, and communities. In the alternative, existing organizations such as the American Planning Association, the National League of Cities, and/or the National Association of Counties could create a program or center focused on RLUIPA and its impact on communities to provide the resources previously discussed.

Notes

1. For example, at least four villages in Rockland County, N.Y., have adopted resolutions seeking congressional repeal of RLUIPA (Airmont, Pomona, Chestnut Ridge, and Wesley Hills). *See Airmont Villager*, April/May 2007, *available at* http://www.airmont.org/newsletters/Villager_200704.pdf. In addition, there is at least one blog dedicated to defeating RLUIPA. *See* http://defeat-rluipa.blogspot.com.
2. *See* Marci Hamilton, *The Five Religion-Related Issues That Should Concern the Future of the Obama Administration*, FINDLAW, Nov. 13, 2008, http://writ.news.findlaw.com/hamilton/20081113.html.
3. Then President-Elect Obama announced the appointment of Melody Barnes as White House director of domestic policy in late November 2008. *See* Capital J, http://blogs.jta.org/politics/

article/2008/11/24/1001178/barnes-gets-thumbs-up-from-ou (last visited Mar. 18, 2009).

4. *City of Boerne v. Flores*, 521 U.S. 507 (1997).
5. 544 U.S. 709 (2005).
6. *See* Michael Boorstein, *For Georgetown "Apostles" a Rowhouse Rebellion*, WASH. POST, Nov. 11, 2006, at A01, *available at* http://www.washingtonpost.com/wp-dyn/content/article/2006/11/10/AR2006111001978.html.
7. Liz Zemba, *Lawsuit Has Nothing to Do with Religious Rights County Says*, TRIBUNE REVIEW, Nov. 13, 2008, http://www.pittsburghlive.com/x/tribunereview/news/fayette/s_598212.html.
8. *Vill. of Euclid v. Ambler Realty Co.*, 272 U.S. 365 (1926).
9. For example, the Becket Fund for Religious Liberty actively recruits religious groups as potential clients to bring RLUIPA cases before the courts.
10. The First Freedom Project, http://www.firstfreedom.gov (last visited Mar. 18, 2009).

Appendix
Religious Land Use and Institutionalized Persons Act of 2000

(Land use provisions only; emphasis added)

§ 2000cc. Protection of land use as religious exercise

(a) Substantial burdens

(1) General rule

No government shall impose or implement a land use regulation in a manner that imposes a substantial burden on the religious exercise of a person, including a religious assembly or institution, unless the government demonstrates that imposition of the burden on that person, assembly, or institution—

(A) is in furtherance of a *compelling governmental interest;* and

(B) is the *least restrictive means* of furthering that compelling governmental interest.

(2) Scope of application

This subsection applies in any case in which—

(A) the substantial burden is imposed in a program or activity that receives Federal financial assistance, even if the burden results from a rule of general applicability;

(B) the substantial burden affects, or removal of that substantial burden would affect, commerce with foreign nations, among the several States, or with Indian tribes, even if the burden results from a rule of general applicability; or

(C) the substantial burden is imposed in the implementation of a land use regulation or system of land use regulations, under which a government makes, or has in place formal or informal procedures or practices that permit the government to make, individualized assessments of the proposed uses for the property involved.

(b) Discrimination and exclusion

(1) Equal terms

No government shall impose or implement a land use regulation in a manner that treats a religious assembly or institution on less than equal terms with a nonreligious assembly or institution.

(2) Nondiscrimination

No government shall impose or implement a land use regulation that discriminates against any assembly or institution on the basis of religion or religious denomination.

(3) Exclusions and limits

No government shall impose or implement a land use regulation that—

(A) totally excludes religious assemblies from a jurisdiction; or

(B) unreasonably limits religious assemblies, institutions, or structures within a jurisdiction.

§ 2000cc–2. Judicial relief

(a) Cause of action: A person may assert a violation of this chapter as a claim or defense in a judicial proceeding and obtain appropriate relief against a government. Standing to assert a claim or defense under this section shall be governed by the general rules of standing under article III of the Constitution.

(b) Burden of persuasion: If a plaintiff produces prima facie evidence to support a claim alleging a violation of the Free Exercise Clause or a violation of section 2000cc of this title, the government shall bear the burden of persuasion on any element of the claim, except that the plaintiff shall bear the burden of persuasion on whether the law (including a regulation) or government practice that is challenged by the claim substantially burdens the plaintiff's exercise of religion.

(c) Full faith and credit: Adjudication of a claim of a violation of section 2000cc of this title in a non-Federal forum shall not be entitled to full faith and credit in a Federal court unless the claimant had a full and fair adjudication of that claim in the non-Federal forum.

. . .

(g) Limitation: If the only jurisdictional basis for applying a provision of this chapter is a claim that a substantial burden by a government on religious exercise affects, or that removal of that substantial burden would affect, commerce with foreign nations, among the several States, or with Indian tribes, the provision shall not apply if the government demonstrates that all substantial burdens on, or the removal of all substantial burdens from, similar religious exercise throughout the Nation would not lead in the aggregate to a substantial effect on commerce with foreign nations, among the several States, or with Indian tribes.

§ 2000cc–3. Rules of construction

(a) Religious belief unaffected: Nothing in this chapter shall be construed to authorize any government to burden any religious belief.

(b) Religious exercise not regulated: Nothing in this chapter shall create any basis for restricting or burdening religious exercise or for claims against a religious organization including any religiously affiliated school or university, not acting under color of law.

(c) Claims to funding unaffected: Nothing in this chapter shall create or preclude a right of any religious organization to receive funding or other assistance from a government, or of any person to receive government funding for a religious activity, but this chapter may require a government to incur expenses in its own operations to avoid imposing a substantial burden on religious exercise.

(d) Other authority to impose conditions on funding unaffected: Nothing in this chapter shall—

(1) authorize a government to regulate or affect, directly or indirectly, the activities or policies of a person other than a

government as a condition of receiving funding or other assistance; or

(2) restrict any authority that may exist under other law to so regulate or affect, except as provided in this chapter.

(e) Governmental discretion in alleviating burdens on religious exercise: A government may avoid the preemptive force of any provision of this chapter by changing the policy or practice that results in a substantial burden on religious exercise, by retaining the policy or practice and exempting the substantially burdened religious exercise, by providing exemptions from the policy or practice for applications that substantially burden religious exercise, or by any other means that eliminates the substantial burden.

(f) Effect on other law: With respect to a claim brought under this chapter, proof that a substantial burden on a person's religious exercise affects, or removal of that burden would affect, commerce with foreign nations, among the several States, or with Indian tribes, shall not establish any inference or presumption that Congress intends that any religious exercise is, or is not, subject to any law other than this chapter.

(g) Broad construction: This chapter shall be construed in favor of a broad protection of religious exercise, to the maximum extent permitted by the terms of this chapter and the Constitution.

(h) No preemption or repeal: Nothing in this chapter shall be construed to preempt State law, or repeal Federal law, that is equally as protective of religious exercise as, or more protective of religious exercise than, this chapter.

(i) Severability: If any provision of this chapter or of an amendment made by this chapter, or any application of such provision to any person or circumstance is held to be unconstitutional, the remainder of this chapter, the amendments made by this chapter, and the application of the provision to any other person or circumstance shall not be affected.

§ 2000cc–4. Establishment Clause unaffected

Nothing in this chapter shall be construed to affect, interpret, or in any way address that portion of the first amendment to the Constitution prohibiting laws respecting an establishment of religion (referred to in this section as the "Establishment Clause").

Granting government funding, benefits, or exemptions, to the extent permissible under the Establishment Clause, shall not constitute a violation of this chapter. In this section, the term "granting," used with respect to government funding, benefits, or exemptions, does not include the denial of government funding, benefits, or exemptions.

§ 2000cc–5. Definitions

In this chapter:

(1) Claimant

The term "claimant" means a person raising a claim or defense under this chapter.

(2) Demonstrates

The term "demonstrates" means meets the burdens of going forward with the evidence and of persuasion.

(3) Free Exercise Clause

The term "Free Exercise Clause" means that portion of the First Amendment to the Constitution that proscribes laws prohibiting the free exercise of religion.

(4) Government

The term "government"—

(A) means—

(i) a State, county, municipality, or other governmental entity created under the authority of a State;

(ii) any branch, department, agency, instrumentality, or official of an entity listed in clause (i); and

(iii) any other person acting under color of State law; and

(B) for the purposes of sections 2000cc–2 (b) and 2000cc–3 of this title, includes the United States, a branch, department, agency, instrumentality, or official of the United States, and any other person acting under color of Federal law.

(5) Land use regulation

The term "land use regulation" means a zoning or landmarking law, or the application of such a law, that limits or restricts a claimant's use or development of land (including a structure affixed to land), if the claimant has an ownership, leasehold, easement, servitude, or other property interest in the regulated land or a contract or option to acquire such an interest.

(6) Program or activity

The term "program or activity" means all of the operations of any entity as described in paragraph (1) or (2) of section 2000d–4a of this title.

(7) Religious exercise

(A) In general

The term "religious exercise" includes any exercise of religion, whether or not compelled by, or central to, a system of religious belief.

(B) Rule

The use, building, or conversion of real property for the purpose of religious exercise shall be considered to be religious exercise of the person or entity that uses or intends to use the property for that purpose.

Table of Cases

Index